WeightWa

Recipes in 45 minutes

D0245513

Midweek Meals

Pı

Dych

First published in Great Britain by Simon & Schuster UK Ltd, 2013
A CBS Company

Weight Watchers Publications: Jane Griffiths, Linda Palmer and Nina McKerlie.

Recipes written by: Sue Ashworth, Sue Beveridge, Tamsin Burnett-Hall,
Cas Clarke, Siân Davies, Roz Denny, Nicola Graimes, Becky Johnson,
Kim Morphew, Joy Skipper, Penny Stephens and Wendy Veale as well
as Weight Watchers Leaders and Members.

Photography by: Iain Bagwell, Steve Baxter, Steve Lee, Juliet Piddington
and William Shaw.
Project editor: Nicki Lampon.
Design and typesetting: Martin Lampon.

Colour reproduction by Dot Gradations Ltd, UK.
Printed and bound in China.

A CIP catalogue for this book is available from the British Library

ISBN 978-1-47111-086-3

1 2 3 4 5 6 7 8 9 10

Pictured on the title page: Stir-fry prawn curry p90.
Pictured on the Introduction: Quick turkey cottage pie p26, Beef and wild mushroom
stroganoff p62, Spicy cod and sausage kebabs p102.

WeightWatchers®

Recipes in 45 minutes or less

Midweek Meals

SIMON &
SCHUSTER
ILLUSTRATED

London · New York · Sydney · Toronto · New Delhi

A CBS COMPANY

Weight Watchers **ProPoints** Weight Loss System is a simple way to lose weight. As part of the Weight Watchers **ProPoints** plan you'll enjoy eating delicious, healthy, filling foods that help to keep you feeling satisfied for longer and in control of your portions.

🅥 This symbol denotes a vegetarian recipe and assumes that, where relevant, free range eggs, vegetarian cheese, vegetarian virtually fat free fromage frais, vegetarian low fat crème fraîche and vegetarian low fat yogurts are used. Virtually fat free fromage frais, low fat crème fraîche and low fat yogurts may contain traces of gelatine so they are not always vegetarian. Please check the labels.

❄ This symbol denotes a dish that can be frozen. Unless otherwise stated, you can freeze the finished dish for up to 3 months. Defrost thoroughly and reheat until the dish is piping hot throughout.

Recipe notes

Egg size: Medium sized, unless otherwise stated.

Raw eggs: Only the freshest eggs should be used. Pregnant women, the elderly and children should avoid recipes with eggs that are not fully cooked or raw.

All fruits and vegetables: Medium sized, unless otherwise stated.

Stock: Stock cubes are used in recipes, unless otherwise stated. These should be prepared according to packet instructions.

Recipe timings: These are approximate and meant to be guidelines. Please note that the preparation time includes all the steps up to and following the main cooking time(s).

Microwaves: Timings and temperatures are for a standard 800 W microwave. If necessary, adjust your own microwave.

Low fat spread: Where a recipe states to use a low fat spread, a light spread with a fat content of no less than 38% should be used.

Low fat soft cheese: Where low fat soft cheese is specified in a recipe, this refers to soft cheese with a fat content of less than 5%.

Contents

Introduction

There is never much time during the week to produce a tasty and healthy meal. But with the help of Weight Watchers you can produce beautiful food in just 45 minutes or less. Perfect for the busy cook, *Midweek Meals* is full of recipes from the best of Weight Watchers cookbooks, all easy to follow and producing fabulous food that you wouldn't believe you could cook so quickly.

Try Sweetcorn and Crab Soup or Cheesy Chicken Goujons for a light meal, tempt the family with Vegetable Biryani or Minced Beef, Beans and Pasta Bake or finish off a meal with a Chocolate Roulade or French Apple Tarts. Whatever you choose, there is plenty here to excite your tastebuds. So get cooking for your family and friends and you'll soon be producing amazing *Midweek Meals*.

About Weight Watchers

For more than 40 years Weight Watchers has been helping people around the world to lose weight using a long term sustainable approach. Weight Watchers successful weight loss system is based on four tried and trusted principles:

- Eating healthily
- Being more active
- Adjusting behaviour to help weight loss
- Getting support in weekly meetings

Our unique ***ProPoints*** system empowers you to manage your food plan and make wise recipe choices for a healthier, happier you.

To find out more about Weight Watchers and the ***ProPoints*** values
for these recipes contact Customer Service on 0845 345 1500.

Storing and freezing

Making meals ahead of time and storing and freezing them is one of the keys to producing healthy tasty meals during a busy week. Many dishes store well in the fridge, but make sure you use them up within a day or two. Some can also be frozen. Try making double the quantity when you cook a recipe and storing the extra portions in the freezer. This way you'll always have a fantastic selection of meals that you can pull out and reheat at the end of a busy day. However, it is important to make sure you know how to freeze safely.

- Wrap any food to be frozen in rigid containers or strong freezer bags. This is important to stop foods contaminating each other or getting freezer burn.
- Label the containers or bags with the contents and date – your freezer should have a star marking that tells you how long you can keep different types of frozen food.
- Never freeze warm food – always let it cool completely first.
- Never freeze food that has already been frozen and defrosted.
- Freeze food in portions, then you can take out as little or as much as you need each time.
- Defrost what you need in the fridge, making sure you put anything that might have juices, such as meat, on a covered plate or in a container.
- Fresh food, such as raw meat and fish, should be wrapped and frozen as soon as possible.
- Most fruit and vegetables can be frozen by open freezing. Lay them out on a tray, freeze until solid and then pack them into bags.
- Some vegetables, such as peas, broccoli and broad beans, can be blanched first by cooking for 2 minutes in boiling water. Drain, refresh under cold water and then freeze once cold.

- Fresh herbs are great frozen – either seal leaves in bags or, for soft herbs such as basil and parsley, chop finely and add to ice cube trays with water. These are great for dropping into casseroles or soups straight from the freezer.

Some things cannot be frozen. Whole eggs do not freeze well, but yolks and whites can be frozen separately. Vegetables with a high water content, such as salad leaves, celery and cucumber, will not freeze. Fried foods will be soggy if frozen, and sauces such as mayonnaise will separate when thawed and should not be frozen.

Shopping hints and tips

Always buy the best ingredients you can afford. If you are going to cook healthy meals, it is worth investing in some quality ingredients that will really add flavour to your dishes. When buying meat, choose lean cuts of meat or lean mince, and if you are buying precooked sliced meat, buy it fresh from the deli counter.

When you're going around the supermarket it's tempting to pick up foods you like and put them in your trolley without thinking about how you will use them. So, a good plan is to decide what dishes you want to cook before you go shopping, check your store cupboard and make a list of what you need. You'll save time by not drifting aimlessly around the supermarket picking up what you fancy.

We've added a checklist here for some of the store cupboard ingredients used in this book. Just add fresh ingredients in your regular shop and you'll be ready to cook the wonderful recipes in *Midweek Meals*.

Store cupboard checklist

- [ ] almonds, flaked
- [ ] apricots, canned in natural juice
- [ ] artificial sweetener
- [ ] beans, canned
- [ ] breadcrumbs, dried natural
- [ ] chick peas, canned
- [ ] chilli powder
- [ ] chilli sauce
- [ ] Chinese five spice
- [ ] cinnamon, ground
- [ ] cocoa powder
- [ ] cooking spray, calorie controlled
- [ ] coriander, ground
- [ ] cornflour
- [ ] couscous, dried
- [ ] crab meat, canned
- [ ] cumin (seeds and ground)
- [ ] curry (powder and paste)
- [ ] fennel seeds
- [ ] fish sauce
- [ ] flour, plain white
- [ ] harissa
- [ ] herbs, dried
- [ ] honey, clear
- [ ] horseradish sauce
- [ ] lentils, canned green
- [ ] mango slices, canned in natural juice
- [ ] mint jelly
- [ ] mustard (Dijon and wholegrain)
- [ ] mustard seeds
- [ ] noodles, dried
- [ ] nutmeg
- [ ] oil, olive
- [ ] oyster sauce
- [ ] paprika, smoked
- [ ] passata
- [ ] pasta, dried
- [ ] pear halves, canned in natural juice
- [ ] peppercorns
- [ ] pesto
- [ ] pineapple chunks, canned in natural juice
- [ ] pizza base mix
- [ ] polenta, dried
- [ ] porcini mushrooms, dried
- [ ] rice, dried (brown, basmati and risotto)
- [ ] salt
- [ ] soy sauce
- [ ] sponge fingers
- [ ] stock cubes
- [ ] sugar (caster, demerara and light brown)
- [ ] sweetcorn, canned
- [ ] tomato purée
- [ ] tomatoes, canned
- [ ] tuna, canned in brine
- [ ] turmeric
- [ ] vanilla extract
- [ ] vinegar (balsamic and rice wine)
- [ ] Worcestershire sauce

Perfect poultry

Honey and mustard chicken salad

Serves 4
228 calories per serving
Takes 35 minutes

500 g (1 lb 2 oz) new potatoes, scrubbed and quartered

200 g (7 oz) asparagus, cut into 2.5 cm (1 inch) lengths

2 x 150 g (5½ oz) skinless boneless chicken breasts

2 teaspoons clear honey

2 tablespoons wholegrain mustard

calorie controlled cooking spray

1 garlic clove, crushed

a large bunch of watercress, washed

200 g (7 oz) cherry tomatoes, halved

salt and freshly ground black pepper

For the dressing

1 tablespoon wholegrain mustard

2 tablespoons virtually fat free plain fromage frais

1 teaspoon clear honey

A fresh and filling warm salad.

1 Bring a large lidded pan of water to boil, add the potatoes and cook for 15 minutes, or until tender. About 5 minutes before the end of the cooking time place the asparagus on top and cover the pan. Drain the cooked asparagus and potatoes together.

2 Meanwhile slice the chicken horizontally to make two thin breast fillets. Put in a small bowl with the honey, mustard and seasoning and leave for 10 minutes to marinate. Preheat the grill and line the grill pan with foil.

3 Heat a large non stick pan and spray with the cooking spray. Stir-fry the garlic for a few seconds and then add the potatoes. Season and stir-fry for 5 minutes, until browned on the edges. Tip into a large bowl.

4 Grill the chicken for 4–5 minutes on each side, until cooked through and golden, then slice into strips.

5 Place the watercress on four serving plates and, in a small bowl, mix together the dressing ingredients with 2 tablespoons of water. Season.

6 Add the chicken strips, cherry tomatoes and asparagus to the cooked potatoes and pour over the dressing. Gently fold together and then pile on top of the watercress to serve.

Fruity chicken couscous

Serves 2
460 calories per serving
Takes 25 minutes

200 ml (7 fl oz) vegetable or chicken stock

½ teaspoon ground coriander

½ teaspoon Madras curry powder

180 g (6½ oz) canned apricot halves in natural juice, drained, chopped and juice reserved

125 g (4½ oz) dried couscous

1 small carrot, peeled and grated

1 small courgette, grated

200 g (7 oz) skinless cooked chicken breast fillets

1 teaspoon harissa

15 g (½ oz) toasted flaked almonds

1 tablespoon chopped fresh parsley, to garnish

Couscous is a staple throughout North Africa but has now become a popular grain in Europe. In 'hot' pursuit is harissa, a fiery paste of chilli pepper and garlic, used in Moroccan and Tunisian cooking.

1 In a small pan bring the stock, with the spices, to simmering point. Remove from the heat, stir in 3 tablespoons of the reserved apricot juice, the couscous, carrot and courgette. Cover and leave for 5 minutes to absorb the liquid.

2 Score the cooked chicken fillets with a sharp knife and rub in the harissa. Heat the chicken up, either by following the packet instructions for the microwave, or by placing them under a medium-high grill for 4–5 minutes.

3 Stir the apricots and almonds into the couscous with a fork. Divide between two plates and arrange the hot chicken on top. Garnish with the parsley.

Tip... This is really delicious served with a mint, cucumber and low fat natural yogurt raita.

Korma turkey tartlets

Serves 4
254 calories per serving
Takes 30 minutes

100 g (3½ oz) asparagus tips
half a kettleful of boiling water
8 x 15 g (½ oz) sheets filo
    pastry, measuring
    30 x 40 cm (12 x 16 inches)
calorie controlled cooking
    spray
225 g (8 oz) cooked skinless
    turkey breast, diced
1 egg, beaten
125 ml (4 fl oz) light single
    cream
1 tablespoon korma spice
    powder
25 g (1 oz) flaked almonds

Serve with a salad and 100 g (3½ oz) boiled new potatoes per person.

1 Preheat the oven to Gas Mark 5/190°C/fan oven 170°C. Put the asparagus tips into a small saucepan and cover with the boiling water. Bring back to the boil, drain immediately and plunge the asparagus tips into cold water. Drain again and dry with kitchen towel. Set aside.

2 Take one sheet of filo pastry and spray with the cooking spray. Fold in half to make a small rectangle measuring 15 x 20 cm (6 x 8 inches). Repeat with all the remaining sheets to make eight small rectangles in total. Spray one small rectangle with the cooking spray and then top with another rectangle to make a stack. Repeat to make four small stacks of two sheets each.

3 Spray a four hole non stick Yorkshire pudding tin with the cooking spray. Line each hole with one stack of pastry, crumpling up the edges to make a lip. Divide the turkey between the pastry cases.

4 Mix together the egg, cream and korma spice powder. Pour a little over each pastry case, scatter over the almonds and top each with the asparagus tips. Bake in the oven for 20 minutes until golden and set.

Tempting Thai turkey

Serves 4

305 calories per serving

Takes 15 minutes to prepare,
15 minutes to cook

125 g (4½ oz) dried Thai
stir-fry rice noodles

a kettleful of boiling water

calorie controlled cooking
spray

450 g (1 lb) skinless boneless
turkey breasts, cut into
strips

100 g (3½ oz) button
mushrooms, halved

2 carrots, peeled and cut into
matchsticks

2 onions, sliced

1 green pepper, de-seeded and
sliced

1 red pepper, de-seeded and
sliced

100 ml (3½ fl oz) oyster sauce

salt and freshly ground black
pepper

This recipe is simply delicious.

1 Place the noodles in a bowl, pour over boiling water and soak according to the packet instructions. Drain thoroughly.

2 Meanwhile, heat a wok or large non stick frying pan and spray with the cooking spray. Add the turkey strips and stir-fry over a high heat for 3–4 minutes, until browned. Remove and set aside.

3 Add all the vegetables to the wok or frying pan and stir-fry for 4–5 minutes. Add the cooked turkey and oyster sauce and then the noodles.

4 Cook over a low heat, stirring occasionally, until the noodles are heated through. Season to taste and serve.

Variations... Use any vegetables you like, such as broccoli, courgettes, spring onions and cauliflower.

Use chicken instead of turkey.

Cheesy chicken goujons

Serves 4
239 calories per serving
Takes 20 minutes
❄ (before cooking)

4 x 125 g (4½ oz) skinless chicken breast fillets
1 egg, beaten
2 medium slices white or wholemeal bread
50 g (1¾ oz) finely grated Parmesan cheese
calorie controlled cooking spray
salt and freshly ground black pepper

These extra tasty chicken goujons are great for sharing.

1 Preheat the oven to Gas Mark 7/220°C/fan oven 200°C. Slice each chicken breast into seven or eight finger width strips.

2 Beat the egg, with seasoning, in a shallow bowl. Whizz the bread to crumbs in a food processor and mix with the grated Parmesan on a large plate.

3 Dip the chicken strips first in the egg and then in the cheesy crumbs to coat. Place on a non stick baking tray that has been lightly sprayed with the cooking spray and mist the chicken goujons with a little more spray. Bake for 10–12 minutes until crisp, golden and cooked through.

Mango and lime chicken

Serves 4
458 calories per serving
Takes 20 minutes
❄ (cooked chicken only)

400 g (14 oz) mango slices in natural juice, drained and 100 ml (3½ fl oz) juice reserved
grated zest and juice of a lime
1 tablespoon clear honey
½ x 25 g packet fresh coriander, leaves only
4 x 165 g (5¾ oz) skinless boneless chicken breasts, halved through the middle
250 g (9 oz) dried Thai jasmine rice
salt and freshly ground black pepper

This fruity, chargrilled chicken is delicious served with a simple tomato and cucumber salad.

1 Put the mango slices, reserved mango juice, lime zest and juice, honey and coriander in a food processor, or use a hand blender, and whizz until nearly puréed. Season. Put half of the sauce into a shallow dish and the remaining half into a small serving bowl.

2 Put the chicken in the shallow dish and turn to coat in the marinade.

3 Bring a pan of water to the boil, add the rice and cook for 10–12 minutes, or according to the packet instructions, until al dente.

4 Meanwhile, heat a non stick griddle pan until hot and cook the chicken breasts for 10 minutes or until cooked through and lightly charred.

5 Drain the rice and divide between four plates. Slice each piece of chicken breast into three and then serve on top of the rice with the reserved mango sauce.

Quick turkey cottage pie

Serves 4

265 calories per serving

Takes 10 minutes to prepare,
  20 minutes to cook

**500 g (1 lb 2 oz) potatoes,
  peeled and cubed**

**4 tablespoons hot skimmed
  milk**

**1 tablespoon chopped fresh
  parsley or ¼ teaspoon
  grated nutmeg (optional)**

**500 g (1 lb 2 oz) minced
  turkey**

**calorie controlled cooking
  spray**

2 garlic cloves, crushed

**½ teaspoon dried thyme,
  oregano or mixed herbs**

4 spring onions, chopped

1 tablespoon plain white flour

500 ml (18 fl oz) chicken stock

**1 tablespoon dried natural
  breadcrumbs**

**salt and freshly ground black
  pepper**

*This wholesome and satisfying supper dish is great served
with peas and carrots. It's wonderful for all the family and
is perfect for a cosy evening meal.*

1 Bring a pan of water to the boil, add the potatoes and
cook for 10–12 minutes, until just tender. Drain well and then
mash them until smooth.

2 Beat in the hot milk, parsley or nutmeg, if using, and
seasoning. Set the mash aside.

3 Meanwhile, heat a large non stick frying pan and add the
turkey in small amounts, stirring quickly to break it up. Spray
the mince with the cooking spray and cook until it becomes
crumbly.

4 Add the garlic, herbs and spring onions. Cook for
2 minutes and then sprinkle in the flour and mix it in. Stir in
the stock and raise the heat. Simmer for 10 minutes until the
mixture has thickened and reduced down. Season well.

5 Preheat the grill to medium high. Spoon the mince mixture
into a flameproof dish. Spoon over the potatoes, spreading
them evenly with a fork, and sprinkle over the breadcrumbs.

6 Place the dish under the grill until the top turns lightly
golden. Serve on four warmed plates.

Variation... For an even quicker meal, serve the mince on
its own with the potatoes, plain boiled and sprinkled with
chopped parsley.

Chicken, sage and basil parcels

Serves 4

320 calories per serving

Takes 15 minutes to prepare,
30 minutes to cook

**4 x 175 g (6 oz) skinless
boneless chicken breasts**

2 garlic cloves, crushed

**1 tablespoon chopped fresh
sage**

**1 tablespoon chopped fresh
basil**

**4 tablespoons fresh white
breadcrumbs**

**1 tablespoon red or green
pesto**

12 fresh sage leaves

12 fresh basil leaves

2 tablespoons olive oil

**1 red pepper, de-seeded and
cut into large chunks**

**1 yellow pepper, de-seeded
and cut into large chunks**

2 courgettes, cut into chunks

8 small tomatoes

**salt and freshly ground black
pepper**

You will need cocktail sticks to secure these lovely parcels.

1 Preheat the oven to Gas Mark 5/190°C/fan oven 170°C.

2 Lay the chicken breasts on a work surface and use a sharp knife to cut a pocket into them. Season.

3 Mix together the garlic, chopped sage and basil, breadcrumbs and pesto, adding a little water if needed to mix to a stiff paste. Spread into the pockets in the chicken and then lay a few sage and basil leaves on top of the filling. Close the pockets and secure with string or cocktail sticks.

4 Heat one tablespoon of olive oil in a frying pan and add the chicken parcels, cooking and turning them over a medium-high heat for about 3 minutes to brown and seal them.

5 Add the remaining oil to a roasting tin and put the peppers and courgettes into it. Arrange the chicken breasts on top and transfer to the oven. Roast for 30 minutes, or until the chicken is tender, adding the tomatoes to the roasting tin for the final 10 minutes. Serve the chicken parcels with the vegetables.

Cheese-topped turkey steaks

Serves 2
265 calories per serving
Takes 25 minutes

2 x 125 g (4½ oz) skinless
  boneless turkey steaks
50 g (1¾ oz) half fat Cheddar
  cheese, grated
25 g (1 oz) fresh white
  breadcrumbs
1 small Cox or Granny Smith
  apple, peeled, cored and
  chopped finely
2 walnut halves, chopped
  coarsely
a pinch of dried sage
salt and freshly ground black
  pepper

*Apple and cheese makes a tasty topping for turkey. Serve
with steamed green vegetables.*

1 Place the steaks between two sheets of greaseproof paper
and flatten them out to approximately 15 mm (⅝ inch) thick.
(This helps speed up the cooking time and gives the impression
of a larger portion.) Preheat the grill to medium high and line
the grill pan with foil.

2 Mix together the cheese, breadcrumbs, apple, walnuts and
sage. Season to taste.

3 Grill the turkey steaks for 4–5 minutes on each side. Spread
the topping mixture evenly over each steak. Continue to cook
for a further 2–3 minutes, until the cheesy breadcrumb mixture
turns golden brown. Serve.

Cheat's biryani

Serves 2
363 calories per serving
Takes 30 minutes

60 g (2 oz) dried basmati rice
1 chicken stock cube,
   crumbled
6 cardamom pods
calorie controlled cooking
   spray
1 onion, sliced
1 cm (½ inch) fresh root
   ginger, grated
2 teaspoons curry paste
200 g canned or cooked
   leftover vegetables, diced
   (e.g. green beans, peppers,
   carrots)
200 g (7 oz) skinless cooked
   tikka or tandoori chicken
   fillets, cut into small pieces
15 g (½ oz) flaked almonds,
   to serve

This has all the flavour of a traditional biryani but is far quicker and easier to make.

1 Bring a pan of water to the boil, add the rice, stock cube and cardamom pods and cook for 15 minutes.

2 Meanwhile, heat a non stick frying pan or wok, spray with the cooking spray and sauté the onion for 3 minutes. Stir in the ginger.

3 Add the curry paste, vegetables and chicken pieces and cook for 5 minutes to make sure they are heated through.

4 Drain the rice when ready, removing the cardamom pods. Stir the rice into the pan. Mix well and serve immediately, sprinkled with the flaked almonds.

Tip... Before adding the vegetables and chicken pieces, allow the spiced rice to cool. Then add the chicken and vegetables. Keep refrigerated and you have an ideal curried rice salad for your lunch box.

Chicken cordon bleu

Serves 4

232 calories per serving

Takes 10 minutes to prepare,
15–20 minutes to cook

4 x 165 g (5¾ oz) skinless boneless chicken breasts

100 g (3½ oz) low fat soft cheese with garlic and herbs

25 g (1 oz) stoned black olives in brine, drained and chopped finely

2 fresh rosemary sprigs, each cut in half

8 x 10 g (¼ oz) smoked wafer thin ham

calorie controlled cooking spray

salt and freshly ground black pepper

In the traditional version of this dish, the ham would be in the middle with the cheese, but putting it on the outside helps to keep the chicken moist and stops the filling from oozing out. Serve with 100 g (3½ oz) new potatoes per person and a mixed green salad.

1 Preheat the oven to Gas Mark 6/200°C/fan oven 180°C. Cut a pocket into the thickest part of each chicken breast. Mix together the soft cheese, olives and seasoning. Use to fill each chicken pocket.

2 Put half a sprig of rosemary on top of each chicken breast and then seal the pocket and hold the rosemary in place with two slices of ham like a plaster. Spray with the cooking spray, transfer to a non stick baking tray or roasting tin and bake in the oven for 15–20 minutes until cooked. Serve immediately.

Malaysian turkey curry

Serves 4
261 calories per serving
Takes 18 minutes
❄

calorie controlled cooking
spray
1 onion, sliced finely
1 garlic clove, crushed
1 teaspoon fennel seeds,
crushed
1 green pepper, de-seeded and
diced
500 g (1 lb 2 oz) lean minced
turkey
2 tablespoons Madras curry
powder
1 teaspoon ground ginger
1 courgette, grated
2 x 150 g pots low fat tropical
yogurt
salt and freshly ground black
pepper

Choose a tropical yogurt such as pineapple or mango to give this dish a truly exotic taste. Enjoy with 60 g (2 oz) dried brown rice per person, cooked according to the packet instructions, and a herb salad.

1 Heat a wide, lidded, non stick saucepan and spray with the cooking spray. Cook the onion, garlic, fennel seeds and pepper for 3–4 minutes. Add the minced turkey and cook for a further 3 minutes, stirring until brown.

2 Stir in the curry powder, ginger and courgette. Cover and cook gently for 5 minutes, stirring occasionally. Gradually stir in the yogurt, season and serve immediately.

Chicken noodles

Serves 4

315 calories per serving

Takes 15 minutes to prepare,
15 minutes to cook

200 g (7 oz) dried rice noodles

a kettleful of boiling water

**calorie controlled cooking
spray**

**a bunch of spring onions,
sliced**

4 garlic cloves, sliced thinly

**200 g (7 oz) skinless boneless
chicken breast, sliced thinly**

150 g (5½ oz) beansprouts

**2 large carrots, peeled and cut
into matchsticks**

**150 g (5½ oz) mange tout,
sliced thinly**

**1 red pepper, de-seeded and
sliced finely**

4 tablespoons soy sauce

**1 tablespoon Worcestershire
sauce**

**100 ml (3½ fl oz) vegetable or
chicken stock**

2 limes

A quick dish that is delicious without the chicken too.

1 Soak the rice noodles in boiling water according to the packet directions.

2 Spray a wok or large non stick frying pan with the cooking spray and stir-fry the spring onions and garlic for 1–2 minutes, adding a tablespoon of water if necessary to prevent them from sticking. Add the chicken and stir-fry for a few minutes, until browned all over.

3 Add all the other ingredients, including the noodles (but except the limes), and stir-fry for a final few minutes, tossing together to mix everything well.

4 Squeeze over the juice of one lime and cut the other into wedges. Serve the noodles with the lime wedges.

Sweet and sour chicken

Serves 4
375 calories per serving
Takes 30 minutes

Stir-fried strips of chicken taste fabulous in this quick and easy dish.

150 g (5½ oz) dried long grain rice
210 g can pineapple chunks in natural juice
2 teaspoons chilli sauce
2 tablespoons light soy sauce
2 tablespoons seasoned rice vinegar dressing
  or cider vinegar
1 tablespoon light muscovado sugar
1 tablespoon cornflour
2 teaspoons Chinese five spice
1 tablespoon stir-fry oil or vegetable oil
350 g (12 oz) skinless boneless chicken
  breast, cut into chunks
1 large red onion, sliced

1 yellow pepper, de-seeded and cut into
  chunks
100 g (3½ oz) mange tout or sugar snap peas,
  halved
3 celery sticks, sliced
4 tomatoes, sliced into wedges
salt and freshly ground black pepper

To garnish
1 red chilli or ½ red pepper, de-seeded and
  sliced thinly
a handful of chopped fresh coriander or
  parsley

1 Bring a pan of water to the boil, add the rice and cook for about 12 minutes, or until tender.

2 Meanwhile, drain the juice from the pineapple into a small bowl or jug. Add the chilli sauce, soy sauce, seasoned rice vinegar dressing or cider vinegar, sugar, cornflour and Chinese five spice. Set aside.

3 Heat the oil in a wok or large non stick frying pan. Add the chicken, a handful at a time, and stir-fry over a high heat for 3–4 minutes.

continues opposite ▶

Sweet and sour chicken *continued*

4 Add the onion, pepper, mange tout or sugar snap peas and celery. Stir-fry for another 3–4 minutes and then add the tomatoes and pineapple.

5 Give the pineapple juice mixture a good stir and then add it to the wok, stirring until hot and thickened. Season to taste, adding a little more soy sauce and chilli sauce, if you like.

6 Serve with the rice, garnished with the thinly sliced chilli or pepper and fresh coriander or parsley.

⊙ Variation... For a vegetarian version, omit the chicken and use 350 g (12 oz) Quorn Chicken Style Pieces instead.

Spanish rice

Serves 4
368 calories per serving
Takes 30 minutes

250 g (9 oz) dried brown rice

400 g can chopped tomatoes with herbs

200 g (7 oz) cooked skinless boneless chicken breast, sliced

230 g packet seafood selection

150 g (5½ oz) frozen peas

2 teaspoons smoked paprika (optional)

Deliciously satisfying.

1 Bring a pan of water to the boil, add the rice and cook according to the packet instructions. Drain well.

2 Place all the ingredients, including the rice, in a wok or large, lidded, non stick frying pan and heat gently.

3 Add 1 tablespoon of water, cover and simmer for 10 minutes until piping hot. Serve in large bowls.

Tip... Smoked paprika, or pimenton, adds a smoky flavour and is available in most larger supermarkets in the herbs and spice or ethnic foods sections.

Speedy turkey and vegetable pie

Serves 2
413 calories per serving
Takes 35 minutes

300 g (10½ oz) white potatoes, such as Maris Piper, washed and halved

calorie controlled cooking spray

300 g (10½ oz) skinless boneless turkey breast, cut into bite size pieces

1 large leek, sliced thinly

100 g (3½ oz) button mushrooms, sliced thinly

1 teaspoon dried thyme

5 tablespoons vegetable stock

4 tablespoons half fat crème fraîche

1 teaspoon Dijon mustard

salt and freshly ground black pepper

Serve this fast family favourite with your choice of steamed vegetables or a large green salad.

1 Bring a pan of water to the boil, add the potatoes and cook for 15 minutes until tender. Remove with a slotted spoon, leave to dry and then peel. Cut into 5 mm (¼ inch) thick slices.

2 Meanwhile, spray a non stick saucepan with the cooking spray. Add the turkey and cook for 6 minutes, turning occasionally, until golden. Remove and set aside.

3 Spray the pan again and add the leek. Cook for 2 minutes and then add the mushrooms and thyme and cook for a further 2 minutes. Return the turkey to the pan with the stock, crème fraîche and mustard, season and simmer for 2 minutes.

4 Preheat the grill to medium high. Transfer the turkey mixture to an 850 ml (1½ pint) flameproof dish and arrange the potato slices on top. Spray with the cooking spray and grill for 10 minutes until golden. Serve immediately.

Chicken and spring onion burgers

Serves 4
270 calories per serving
Takes 30 minutes

500 g (1 lb 2 oz) minced
chicken or turkey
6 spring onions, chopped
finely
3 garlic cloves, crushed
2 tablespoons chopped fresh
parsley
grated zest and juice of a lime
calorie controlled cooking
spray
salt and freshly ground black
pepper

To serve
4 medium burger buns
2 tablespoons tomato ketchup
salad leaves, tomato and
cucumber

*These little burgers can be made with minced chicken
or turkey and go down a treat with adults and children
alike. Serve with a crisp salad with crunchy hot radishes
and beansprouts or 125 g (4½ oz) low fat oven chips per
person.*

1 Mix together the mince, spring onions, garlic, parsley, lime
zest and seasoning.

2 Using wet hands, shape into four patties. Heat a non stick
frying pan and spray with the cooking spray. Fry the patties for
5–10 minutes on each side until cooked through.

3 Meanwhile, split the buns and toast lightly. Spread each half
with ¼ of a tablespoon of tomato ketchup and then arrange
the salad on the base of each bun and place a burger on top.
Squeeze a little lime juice over, replace the top half of the bun
and serve.

Variation... Use low fat mayonnaise instead of ketchup if
you prefer.

Marvellous meat

Ham, leek and potato soup

Serves 4
145 calories per serving
Takes 30 minutes
❄

This is a wonderfully wholesome soup, ideal for those 'hungry' Saturday lunchtimes when you are never quite sure how many family or friends might pop by.

2 leeks, sliced finely

2 potatoes, peeled, quartered and sliced finely

600 ml (20 fl oz) hot vegetable stock

1 tablespoon cornflour

200 ml (7 fl oz) semi skimmed milk

2 teaspoons Dijon or wholegrain mustard

2 tablespoons chopped fresh parsley or 2 teaspoons dried parsley

150 g (5½ oz) wafer thin smoked ham, cut into pieces

salt and freshly ground black pepper

1 Place the leeks and potatoes in a large lidded saucepan, pour over the hot stock, cover and cook for 10 minutes.

2 Meanwhile, blend the cornflour with the milk. Stir in the mustard and parsley. Add to the potato and leeks, stirring until the mixture thickens slightly. Simmer for a further 10 minutes.

3 Add the ham to the saucepan. Season to taste. Heat gently for another minute or two before serving.

Variation... Replace the ham with wafer thin turkey and substitute the parsley with 1 tablespoon of chopped fresh tarragon or sage.

Puffy pancetta and leek omelette

Serves 4
174 calories per serving
Takes 20 minutes

3 eggs, separated
75 g (2¾ oz) ricotta cheese
2 tablespoons finely chopped
    fresh parsley
75 g (2¾ oz) pancetta, diced
1 leek, sliced finely
75 g (2¾ oz) frozen peas,
    defrosted
calorie controlled cooking
    spray
salt and freshly ground black
    pepper

Pancetta is Italian dry cured bacon. If you would prefer, you can use 75 g (2¾ oz) diced lean back bacon instead.

1 In a large bowl, mix together the egg yolks, 50 g (1¾ oz) of ricotta, the parsley and seasoning. Set aside.

2 Heat a deep non stick frying pan, about 18 cm (7 inches) in diameter, and cook the pancetta for 1–2 minutes until crispy. Remove and drain on kitchen towel. Add the leek to the pan and cook for 3–4 minutes until softened but not coloured. Remove and set aside.

3 In a clean, grease-free bowl, whisk the egg whites until stiff peaks nearly form. Using a metal spoon, carefully fold the egg whites into the ricotta mixture along with half of each of the crispy pancetta, leek and peas until combined.

4 Preheat the grill to medium. Reheat the frying pan and spray with the cooking spray. Pour in the egg mixture and gently cook for 3–4 minutes until golden underneath. While still on the heat, top the omelette with the remaining ricotta, pancetta, leek and peas. Transfer to the grill and cook for 3–4 minutes until golden and puffy. Serve immediately in wedges.

Sheek kebabs

Serves 4
200 calories per serving
Takes 20 minutes
❄

400 g (14 oz) minced lamb
1 egg
3 garlic cloves, crushed
1 teaspoon mint sauce
2 teaspoons paprika
2 teaspoons curry powder
2 teaspoons chilli powder
1 teaspoon turmeric
1 teaspoon ground coriander
1 teaspoon ground cumin
a small bunch of fresh
  coriander, chopped
salt and freshly ground black
  pepper

Serve these tasty and easy kebabs with a large mixed salad.

1 Mix all the ingredients together in a bowl and then divide the mixture into 12 portions. Roll each portion in your hands and then flatten slightly to make 12 kebab shapes.

2 Preheat the grill to medium high. Grill the kebabs for 5 minutes on each side, until cooked through and golden. Serve immediately, allowing three kebabs per person.

Tangy lamb chops with Irish mash

Serves 4

405 calories per serving

Takes 10 minutes to prepare,
20 minutes to cook

❄ (mash only)

**750 g (1 lb 10 oz) potatoes,
peeled and cut into chunks**

150 ml (5 fl oz) skimmed milk

1 teaspoon low fat spread

**4 x 100 g (3½ oz) lamb chump
chops, trimmed of visible fat**

**½ green cabbage, cored and
shredded**

4 spring onions, chopped

freshly grated nutmeg

**4 teaspoons BBQ or brown
sauce**

**salt and freshly ground black
pepper**

*Creamy mashed potato is a great Irish family dish, and
the juicy, tangy glazed lamb in this recipe accompanies it
perfectly. Serve with grilled tomatoes.*

1 Bring a pan of water to the boil, add the potatoes and cook
for about 12 minutes, until tender. Drain well and return them
to the pan. Mash the potatoes until smooth.

2 Heat the milk and low fat spread in a small saucepan.
Add this to the potatoes and mix until you have a creamy
consistency.

3 Meanwhile, preheat the grill to medium high. Season the
lamb chops and grill for about 4 minutes on each side until the
meat is almost firm.

4 While the lamb is grilling, bring another pan of water to the
boil, add the cabbage and cook for 5 minutes. Drain well.

5 Mix the cabbage and spring onions into the mash and
season with nutmeg, salt and pepper to taste. Reheat the mash
gently if necessary.

6 Spread a teaspoon of BBQ or brown sauce on one side of
each lamb chop. Return them to the grill for a further minute
until the glaze bubbles.

7 Divide the mashed potato mixture between four warmed
plates and arrange a chop on top of each.

**Tip... For perfect mashed potatoes, choose a good variety
such as Maris Piper, Désirée or King Edward.**

Honey and mustard pork

Serves 4
275 calories per serving
Takes 25 minutes

450 g (1 lb) swede, peeled and
  diced
450 g (1 lb) carrots, peeled
  and diced
calorie controlled cooking
  spray
4 x 150 g (5½ oz) lean pork
  steaks, trimmed of visible fat
2 tablespoons clear honey
2 tablespoons wholegrain
  mustard
juice of ½ a lemon
salt and freshly ground black
  pepper

*These pork steaks, in a delicious sweet-sharp sauce, need
nothing more than some green cabbage to go with them.*

1 Bring a large lidded pan of water to the boil, add the diced
swede and carrots, cover and simmer for 15–20 minutes until
tender. Drain well, mash roughly and season to taste.

2 When the vegetables have been cooking for about
10 minutes, heat a large non stick frying pan on the hob
and spray with the cooking spray. Season the pork steaks
and brown for 3–4 minutes on each side, depending on their
thickness, or until cooked through.

3 Mix the honey, mustard and lemon juice together and
pour over the pork steaks. Cook for 1 minute more, turning
the pork steaks to glaze them in the sauce. Serve with the
mashed carrot and swede.

Chilli bean beef

Serves 4

264 calories per serving

Takes 10 minutes to prepare,
20 minutes to cook

❄

500 g (1 lb 2 oz) extra lean
minced beef

1 onion, chopped finely

1 teaspoon ground cumin

1 teaspoon hot chilli powder

2 garlic cloves, crushed

400 g can chopped tomatoes

420 g can mixed pulses,
drained and rinsed

200 ml (7 fl oz) beef stock

1 green pepper, de-seeded and
diced

1 yellow pepper, de-seeded
and diced

salt and freshly ground black
pepper

*A quick and easy meal; serve with 60 g (2 oz) dried
brown rice per person, cooked according to the packet
instructions, or a 225 g (8 oz) jacket potato per person,
baked in its skin.*

1 Brown the minced beef and onion in a large, lidded, non
stick pan over a medium heat for 8 minutes, stirring to break
up the meat.

2 Mix in the spices and garlic, cook for 30 seconds and then
add the remaining ingredients and seasoning.

3 Bring to a simmer and cook, partially covered, for
20 minutes.

Minced beef, beans and pasta bake

Serves 4

325 calories per serving

Takes 5 minutes to prepare, 25 minutes to cook

❄

1 onion, chopped

350 g (12 oz) extra lean minced beef

150 ml (5 fl oz) beef stock

227 g can chopped tomatoes

415 g can Weight Watchers from Heinz baked beans

2 teaspoons Worcestershire sauce

1 teaspoon dried mixed herbs

100 g (3½ oz) dried fusilli

salt and freshly ground black pepper

Serve in warmed bowls with steamed cauliflower or broccoli.

1 Heat a large, lidded, non stick saucepan and dry fry the onion with the minced beef for 4–5 minutes until the meat becomes crumbly and browned.

2 Stir in the remaining ingredients. Bring to the boil, cover and simmer gently for 20 minutes, until the pasta is cooked. Season to taste and serve.

 Variation... For a vegetarian option, replace the minced beef with Quorn mince and the beef stock with vegetable stock. Because Quorn does not have a lot of flavour on its own, try adding 1 teaspoon chilli powder or medium curry powder with the Quorn in step 1.

Spaghetti carbonara

Serves 4

530 calories per serving

Takes 5 minutes to prepare,
  15 minutes to cook

350 g (12 oz) dried spaghetti
calorie controlled cooking
  spray
8 lean back bacon rashers
1 garlic clove, chopped finely
1 egg
2 egg whites
100 g (3½ oz) low fat soft
  cheese
25 g packet fresh parsley,
  chopped
salt and freshly ground black
  pepper

*This takes minutes to make with ingredients that are,
hopefully, in your fridge.*

1 Bring a pan of water to the boil, add the pasta and cook
for 10 minutes until cooked, or according to the packet
instructions. Drain.

2 Spray a large non stick pan with the cooking spray and
put over a medium heat. Fry the bacon until crispy – about
5 minutes – and then add the garlic and cook for a further
minute.

3 Add the hot spaghetti to the bacon in the pan and quickly
add the egg, egg whites, soft cheese, a little salt and lots of
pepper and toss together. The heat of the spaghetti should
cook the eggs and very slightly thicken the sauce.

4 Stir in the parsley and serve with more black pepper.

Beef and wild mushroom stroganoff

Serves 4
405 calories per serving
Takes 20 minutes
❄

calorie controlled cooking
spray

2 x 400 g (14 oz) rump steaks,
trimmed of visible fat and
cut into thin strips

4 shallots, sliced in half
lengthways and then into
fine semi-circles

4 garlic cloves, crushed

500 g (1 lb 2 oz) wild
mushrooms or a combination
of wild and field or button
and chestnut mushrooms

a small bunch of fresh thyme,
woody stems removed and
leaves chopped

2 tablespoons tomato purée

2 tablespoons Dijon mustard

a small bunch of fresh parsley,
chopped roughly

200 g (7 oz) half fat crème
fraîche

½ teaspoon paprika

salt and freshly ground black
pepper

Serve this comforting casserole with a sweet potato mash.

1 Heat a large non stick pan and spray with the cooking spray. Fry a handful of the steak pieces, with seasoning, over a high heat until browned all over. Remove to a plate and fry the rest of the meat in batches.

2 Spray the pan again with the cooking spray. Fry the shallots and garlic until soft, adding a little water if necessary to prevent them from sticking.

3 Add the mushrooms, thyme and tomato purée, season and cook, stirring, for 1 minute.

4 Put the steak back in the pan with any juices, the mustard and parsley and mix together. Stir in the crème fraîche and cook on a low heat for 4–5 minutes. Stir in the paprika, check the seasoning and serve.

Tip... To make sweet potato mash, peel and chop approximately 300 g (10½ oz) sweet potatoes. Bring a pan of water to the boil, add the potatoes and cook for 15–20 minutes until tender. Mash with seasoning.

Grilled lamb with garlic beans

Serves 2
530 calories per serving
Takes 25 minutes

4 lean lamb loin chops, trimmed of visible fat
2 teaspoons pesto
2 teaspoons olive oil
2 garlic cloves, sliced thinly
400 g can haricot blanc or other small beans, drained and rinsed
salt and freshly ground black pepper
a small bunch of fresh chives, chopped, to garnish (optional)

This is a useful way to jazz up a can of small beans. Here they are served with grilled lamb chops for a quick supper; just add steamed vegetables of your choice.

1 Heat the grill to high and season the lamb chops. Spread with a little pesto and lay on a foil-lined grill pan. Place under the grill for 3–4 minutes, depending on how well you like them cooked, and then turn over and spread with a little more pesto. Grill for a further 3–4 minutes.

2 Meanwhile, heat the olive oil in a lidded non stick pan and stir-fry the garlic for a few minutes until lightly golden. Add the beans, season, toss together and allow to warm through for a few minutes. Turn off the heat, cover the pan and leave for a minute or two to allow the flavours to mingle.

3 Place a large spoonful of the beans on each plate with two lamb chops and sprinkle with chopped chives, if using, to serve.

Rosemary pork fillet with lemon rice

Serves 4
448 calories per serving
Takes 45 minutes

500 g (1 lb 2 oz) pork fillet, trimmed of visible fat

finely grated zest and juice of a lemon

1½ tablespoons finely chopped fresh rosemary

calorie controlled cooking spray

2 leeks, sliced

250 g (9 oz) dried risotto rice

700 ml (1¼ pints) hot chicken stock

25 g (1 oz) grated Parmesan cheese

freshly ground black pepper

This is a very easy way to cook risotto rice. Serve with slices of courgette, griddled using cooking spray.

1 Preheat the oven to Gas Mark 6/200°C/fan oven 180°C. Drizzle half the lemon juice over the pork and then rub 1 tablespoon of the rosemary and half the lemon zest into the meat. Season with black pepper. Place the pork in a roasting tin, spray with the cooking spray and roast in the oven for 25 minutes or until the juices run clear when the thickest part of the fillet is pierced.

2 Meanwhile, spray a large saucepan with the cooking spray. Add the leeks and cook for 2 minutes and then add the rest of the rosemary and the risotto rice, stirring for 1 minute.

3 Pour in the hot stock and bring to the boil. Simmer, uncovered, for 18 minutes or until the rice is tender. Stir in the cheese, plus the rest of the lemon zest and juice. Season to taste.

4 Carve the pork into thin slices and serve on a bed of the lemon and leek rice.

Tip... If you've got time, before carving the pork into slices, let the pork fillet rest for 5–10 minutes once it has come out of the oven, covered loosely with foil. This will allow the cooking juices that have bubbled up during roasting to be re-absorbed into the meat, so that it will be more tender and moist.

Steak with sweet and sour onions

Serves 2
420 calories per serving
Takes 45 minutes

500 g (1 lb 2 oz) potatoes, peeled and chopped roughly
calorie controlled cooking spray
1 large onion, sliced
250 ml (9 fl oz) beef stock
3 tablespoons sherry vinegar
1½ teaspoons artificial sweetener
2 x 125 g (4½ oz) sirloin steaks, trimmed of visible fat
4 tablespoons skimmed milk, warmed
1½ tablespoons horseradish sauce
salt and freshly ground black pepper

The tangy sweet and sour onions make a delicious accompaniment to steak and creamy mashed potatoes enhanced with horseradish.

1 Bring a pan of water to the boil, add the potatoes and cook for 20 minutes, or until tender.

2 Meanwhile, heat a non stick pan, spray with the cooking spray and fry the onion for 5–6 minutes until browned, adding a splash of stock if necessary to prevent it from sticking.

3 Add the sherry vinegar, stock and sweetener to the browned onions, season and simmer uncovered for 10 minutes until tender and syrupy.

4 Heat a non stick frying pan, season the steaks and spray with the cooking spray. Cook for 3 minutes each side for medium or a little longer for well done.

5 When the potatoes are tender, drain into a colander. Use a potato ricer for the best possible texture, or mash as normal. Mix in the warmed milk, horseradish sauce and seasoning. Serve alongside the steaks, with the sweet and sour onions spooned over.

Lamb and haricot bean fricassee

Serves 4
266 calories per serving
Takes 15 minutes
❄

400 g (14 oz) lean lamb leg steaks, diced

calorie controlled cooking spray

2 bunches spring onions, cut into chunky pieces

2 garlic cloves, crushed

½ teaspoon dried rosemary

150 ml (5 fl oz) vegetable stock

2 x 410 g cans haricot beans, drained and rinsed

2 tablespoons half fat crème fraîche

salt and freshly ground black pepper

Deeply savoury, this hearty fricassee needs only a simple green vegetable such as cabbage to accompany it.

1 Season the lamb, spray a large non stick frying pan with the cooking spray and brown the meat, over a high heat, for 4–5 minutes.

2 Add the spring onions, garlic and rosemary to the frying pan. Cook for 1 minute more, stirring.

3 Mix in the stock and haricot beans and simmer for 3 minutes. Stir in the crème fraîche to make a sauce, check the seasoning and serve.

Middle Eastern meatballs

Serves 4

375 calories per serving

Takes 15 minutes to prepare,
15 minutes to cook

❄

calorie controlled cooking
    spray

1 onion, half chopped and half
    grated

300 ml (10 fl oz) vegetable
    stock

2 wholewheat crispbreads,
    crumbled

500 g (1 lb 2 oz) lean minced
    lamb

½ x 25 g packet fresh
    coriander, stalks chopped
    and leaves reserved

1 teaspoon ground cinnamon

1 teaspoon ground cumin

400 g can chopped tomatoes

410 g can chick peas, drained
    and rinsed

salt and freshly ground black
    pepper

Meatballs are always a popular family meal, but the flavour in this recipe has a real twist. Spoon the meatballs on to a bed of cooked couscous (150 g/5½ oz per person), for the ideal accompaniment.

1 Spray a lidded flameproof casserole dish with the cooking spray. Fry the chopped half of the onion for 2 minutes. Add 3 tablespoons of stock, cover and cook for 2 minutes more.

2 Place the grated onion in a mixing bowl and stir in the crispbread crumbs and 2 tablespoons of stock to moisten them. Add the minced lamb, coriander stalks, ½ teaspoon of the ground cinnamon and season. Mix well and shape into 20 meatballs.

3 Add the cumin, the remaining ½ teaspoon cinnamon, tomatoes, chick peas and the rest of the stock to the casserole and simmer for 5 minutes.

4 Meanwhile, spray a non stick frying pan with the cooking spray and brown the meatballs for 5 minutes, turning to colour them evenly. Gently stir the browned meatballs into the sauce and simmer, uncovered, for 15 minutes. Serve with the coriander leaves scattered over the top.

Olive crusted pork

Serves 2

432 calories per serving

Takes 10 minutes to prepare,
15–20 minutes to cook

**2 x 150 g (5½ oz) lean pork
loin steaks, trimmed of
visible fat**

**calorie controlled cooking
spray**

**2 x 15 g (½ oz) wholewheat
crispbreads**

**60 g (2 oz) stoned green
olives in brine, drained and
chopped**

1 garlic clove, crushed

1 teaspoon Dijon mustard

**1 tablespoon chopped fresh
parsley**

*This topping is a fantastic way to liven up a pork steak
and helps to keep it really moist. Serve with two 60 g
(2 oz) scoops of mashed potato per person and chargrilled
courgettes and peppers.*

1 Preheat the oven to Gas Mark 6/200°C/fan oven 180°C.
Heat a non stick frying pan and spray the pork steaks with the
cooking spray. Cook for 3–4 minutes, turning halfway, until
brown all over. Remove and place on a non stick baking tray.

2 In a food processor, whizz the crispbreads, olives, garlic,
half the mustard and all of the parsley until it forms a coarse
mixture (it will come together).

3 Brush the remaining mustard over one side of each pork
steak and press half the olive mixture on top of each. Bake in
the oven for 15–20 minutes until golden.

Seared beef with amatriciana sauce

Serves 4
373 calories per serving
Takes 25 minutes

calorie controlled cooking
  spray
4 rashers lean back bacon,
  chopped roughly
a bunch of spring onions,
  sliced
4 garlic cloves, crushed
400 g can chopped tomatoes
1 tablespoon fresh thyme
  leaves
100 ml (3½ fl oz) vegetable
  stock
2 x 410 g cans cannellini
  beans, drained and rinsed
450 g (1 lb) lean beef
  escalopes, trimmed of
  visible fat
salt and freshly ground black
  pepper

*This tasty beef in sauce is served with mashed beans – a
lovely change from mashed potato.*

1 To make the sauce, spray a non stick saucepan with the
cooking spray and heat until hot. Fry the bacon for 3 minutes
and then add the spring onions and half the garlic. Cook
for 2 minutes more before stirring in the tomatoes and
seasoning with black pepper. Bring to a simmer and cook
for 8–10 minutes, uncovered, to thicken the sauce.

2 Meanwhile, spray another lidded non stick saucepan with
the cooking spray and fry the remaining garlic and the thyme
for 1–2 minutes. Mix in the stock and the beans. Cover and
simmer for 5 minutes and then mash together with a potato
masher. Season to taste.

3 Spray a non stick frying pan with the cooking spray and pan
fry the beef escalopes for 2 minutes on each side. Make a bed
of bean mash on each plate, sit the beef escalopes on top and
serve with the sauce spooned over.

Lamb cutlets with caramelised minted onions

Serves 2
140 calories per serving
Takes 25 minutes

1 large red or white onion, sliced thinly
a pinch of dried rosemary
2 teaspoons mint jelly
4 x 75 g (2¾ oz) lean lamb cutlets
salt and freshly ground black pepper

Lamb and mint is such a classic combination.

1 Put the onion and rosemary in a small lidded saucepan with 100 ml (3½ fl oz) of water. Bring to a rapid boil. Cover and simmer for 10 minutes.

2 Stir the mint jelly into the onions. Simmer, uncovered, for 5 minutes, stirring occasionally, and then season. Preheat the grill.

3 Grill the cutlets for 2–3 minutes on either side until cooked to your liking. Serve with the sticky minted onions.

Variation... For honey, thyme and balsamic onions, replace the mint jelly with 1 teaspoon clear honey and a few drops of balsamic vinegar. Add 1 teaspoon chopped fresh thyme.

Fantastic fish and seafood

Sweetcorn and crab soup

Serves 4

135 calories per serving

Takes 5 minutes to prepare,
10 minutes to cook

1 egg white
1 teaspoon sesame oil
1.2 litres (2 pints) chicken stock
275 g (9½ oz) frozen sweetcorn or canned sweetcorn, drained
1 tablespoon soy sauce
2 teaspoons chopped fresh root ginger
2 teaspoons cornflour
225 g (8 oz) canned crab meat, drained
freshly ground black pepper
4 spring onions, chopped, to garnish

A delicious soup filled with sweetcorn and crab – great as a starter or even a light lunch.

1 Beat the egg white and sesame oil together and set aside.

2 Bring the stock to the boil in a large pan and add the sweetcorn. Simmer for 5 minutes and then add the soy sauce and ginger. Mix the cornflour to a smooth paste with 2 teaspoons of water and add to the soup. Season with black pepper.

3 Bring the stock back to the boil, lower the heat to a simmer and add the crab meat.

4 Slowly pour in the egg white and sesame oil mixture, stirring constantly. Sprinkle over the spring onions and serve.

Tip... When buying fresh ginger, always select firm, unshrivelled pieces and peel off the skin before use.

Variation... Chicken and sweetcorn soup can be made in the same way – substitute the same amount of cooked shredded chicken for the crab meat.

Potted peppered mackerel

Serves 6
145 calories per serving
Takes 10 minutes
❄

220 g can butter beans, drained and rinsed

200 g (7 oz) peppered mackerel fillets, skinned

1 large red onion, chopped very finely

1 garlic clove, crushed (optional)

finely grated zest and juice of a lemon

1 tablespoon chopped fresh parsley

salt and freshly ground black pepper

To garnish
a few fresh parsley sprigs
lemon slices

This tasty mackerel pâté is sure to become a favourite. Serve on toast with a mixed salad or on a 225 g (8 oz) jacket potato per person, baked in its skin.

1 Tip the beans into a large mixing bowl and use a potato masher or fork to mash to a purée.

2 Flake the mackerel fillets roughly with a fork and then stir into the beans.

3 Add most of the red onion, reserving a little for garnish. Add the garlic, if using, lemon zest and juice and parsley. Season and then mix together thoroughly.

4 Divide the mixture between six small ramekin dishes. Cover and chill until ready to serve, then garnish with parsley sprigs, lemon slices and the reserved red onion.

Tips... For a smooth pâté, whizz together all the ingredients in a food processor or blender for 15 seconds.

For a decorative starter, use the mackerel pâté to fill hollowed-out tomatoes.

Variations... If you prefer, use a drained 190 g can of peppered mackerel instead.

Canned chick peas or cannellini beans can be used instead of butter beans. These are best when puréed in a blender.

Oriental prawn salad

Serves 2

360 calories per serving

Takes 15 minutes

150 g (5½ oz) fine green
  beans, halved

350 g (12 oz) ripe mango,
  peeled, stoned and diced

150 g (5½ oz) beansprouts

4 spring onions, sliced

300 g (10½ oz) cooked peeled
  tiger prawns, defrosted if
  frozen

150 g (5½ oz) leaves from
  a Chinese leaf lettuce,
  shredded

For the dressing:

grated zest and juice of a lime

1 tablespoon clear honey

1 tablespoon fish sauce

2 tablespoons chopped fresh
  coriander

*Succulent prawns mingled with the juicy, sweet flesh of
ripe mango make a perfect combination.*

1 Bring a small pan of water to the boil, add the beans and
cook for 2–3 minutes. Drain and refresh under cold running
water.

2 Toss the mango together with the cooked beans,
beansprouts, spring onions, prawns and Chinese leaf lettuce.

3 Mix together the dressing ingredients and drizzle over the
salad. Toss everything together well and pile the salad into a
serving bowl.

Tip... Although tiger prawns look attractive in this dish,
you can use ordinary cooked peeled prawns as a cheaper
alternative.

Tuna salad pizzas

Serves 2

374 calories per serving

Takes 25 minutes to prepare,
15 minutes to cook

100 g (3½ oz) pizza base mix
20 g (¾ oz) plain white flour
1 red onion, half cut into thin
  rings and the rest chopped
  very finely
1 garlic clove, crushed
200 g can chopped tomatoes
½ teaspoon caster sugar
½ teaspoon dried oregano
2 tablespoons tomato purée
200 g (7 oz) tuna in brine,
  drained
10 stoned black olives in
  brine, drained

To serve
20 g (¾ oz) rocket
2 teaspoons balsamic vinegar

These are great for a lunch or light meal.

1 Preheat the oven to Gas Mark 7/220°C/fan oven 200°C.
Add 75 ml (3 fl oz) of warm water to the pizza base mix and
mix to a smooth dough, or follow the packet instructions. Dust
your work surface with the flour and knead the dough well for
5 minutes.

2 Roll the dough into two rough circles, each about 20 cm
(8 inches) across. Place on non stick baking trays and leave
in a warm place for 10 minutes.

3 Meanwhile, to make the tomato sauce, put the chopped
onion, garlic, tomatoes, sugar, oregano and tomato purée in
a small saucepan. Mix well, bring to a simmer and cook for
10 minutes or until thick.

4 Spread the tomato sauce over the pizzas. Scatter chunky
bits of tuna, the olives and the onion rings over the top. Bake
in the oven for 15 minutes or until crisp.

5 Serve hot, topped with the rocket and drizzled with the
balsamic vinegar.

Grilled cod with spring herbs

Serves 2

260 calories per serving

Takes 15 minutes

2 x 175 g (6 oz) cod steaks

finely grated zest and juice of
½ a lemon

1 teaspoon olive oil

3 tablespoons chopped fresh
herbs, such as dill, chives or
parsley

salt and freshly ground black
pepper

*Use whatever fresh herbs you have on hand to jazz up a
simple piece of fish.*

1 Preheat the grill to medium high. Rinse the cod steaks and
pat them dry with kitchen towel. Line the grill pan with foil and
place the steaks on it.

2 Mix together the lemon zest, lemon juice, olive oil, herbs
and seasoning. Spoon half the mixture over one side of the
fish and grill for 2–3 minutes.

3 Turn the fish over and spoon over the remaining herb
mixture. Grill for a further 2–3 minutes or until cooked
through. Serve at once.

Eastern salmon

Serves 2

247 calories per serving

Takes 5 minutes to prepare,
20 minutes to cook

1 tablespoon soy sauce
½ teaspoon clear honey
½ teaspoon Chinese five spice
2 x 125 g (4½ oz) salmon
fillets

This is so simple but gives plain salmon a fantastic flavour. Serve with a large mixed salad.

1 Preheat the oven to Gas Mark 6/200°C/fan oven 180°C.

2 Mix together the soy sauce, honey and Chinese five spice in a shallow ovenproof dish, just big enough to take the fillets.

3 Roll the salmon fillets in the mixture so that all the sides are coated. Place them skin side down in the dish.

4 Bake in the oven for 20 minutes until the fish is cooked.

Stir-fry prawn curry

Serves 2

195 calories per serving

Takes 10 minutes to prepare,
5 minutes to cook

225 g (8 oz) cooked peeled
tiger prawns

1 tablespoon dry sherry

2 teaspoons light soy sauce

2 teaspoons vegetable or
groundnut oil

1 small onion, chopped
roughly

1 garlic clove, crushed

1 small red or green chilli,
de-seeded and chopped

1 teaspoon finely chopped
fresh root ginger

1 lemongrass stalk, chopped
finely

1 teaspoon Madras curry
paste

½ teaspoon caster sugar

a few fresh coriander sprigs,
to garnish

Serve with 60 g (2 oz) dried noodles per person, cooked according to the packet instructions, or with some fresh steamed vegetables.

1 In a bowl, mix together the prawns, sherry and soy sauce. Cover and leave in a cool place until required. (This can be done several hours before they are needed.)

2 Heat the oil in a wok or large non stick frying pan and stir-fry the onion for 1 minute. Add the garlic, chilli, ginger, lemongrass and curry paste and stir-fry for 1 minute more.

3 Add the prawns, soy sauce and sherry together with the sugar and 2 tablespoons of water. Stir-fry for 2 minutes and then serve immediately, garnished with the coriander.

Tip... Fresh chillies contain oils that can make sensitive skin tingle and eyes smart, so rub your hands with a light coating of cooking oil, which will form a barrier. This makes it easier to wash off these hot oils.

Variation... Replace the prawns with 250 g (9 oz) skinless boneless stir-fry chicken strips.

Fisherman's pot

Serves 4

295 calories per serving

Takes 5 minutes to prepare,
25 minutes to cook

❄

450 g (1 lb) new potatoes,
scrubbed and cut into
quarters

a strip of orange or lemon zest

1 tablespoon chopped fresh
dill, tarragon or chives or
1 teaspoon dried herbs

600 ml (20 fl oz) hot vegetable
stock

4 tablespoons white wine

1 fennel bulb, sliced thinly
(optional)

225 g (8 oz) skinless salmon
fillets, cut into 8 chunks

225 g (8 oz) skinless haddock
fillets, cut into 8 chunks

4 tablespoons half fat crème
fraîche

salt and freshly ground black
pepper

*Choose the best fresh fish available for this tasty catch.
Delicious served with puréed broccoli (see Tips) or fresh
green beans.*

1 Place the potatoes, orange or lemon zest, herbs, stock, wine
and fennel, if using, in a large lidded saucepan, cover and bring
to the boil. Simmer for 15–20 minutes or until the vegetables
are tender.

2 Add the chunks of fish and cook for 3 minutes. Stir in the
crème fraîche and season to taste.

Tips... For puréed broccoli, simply cook until tender and
then whizz in a blender until smooth. Season well.

This recipe is ideal for entertaining, as the preparation
is minimal and it needs little attention during cooking.
However, for an everyday meal, you may want to omit the
crème fraîche and wine.

Mussels with tarragon

Serves 4
185 calories per serving
Takes 20 minutes

calorie controlled cooking
   spray
4 large shallots, chopped
   finely
2 garlic cloves, chopped finely
2 kg (4 lb 8 oz) fresh mussels,
   cleaned (see Tip)
300 ml (10 fl oz) vegetable
   stock
a small bunch of fresh
   tarragon, tough stalks
   removed, chopped
salt and freshly ground black
   pepper

*This makes a super fast supper. Serve with a 50 g (1¾ oz)
crusty bread roll per person to mop up the juices.*

1 Spray a large, lidded, non stick saucepan with the cooking
spray and fry the shallots and garlic until softened, adding a
little water if necessary to prevent them from sticking.

2 Add the mussels and stock and cover the pan. Cook over
a high heat for 3–4 minutes, or until all the mussels have
opened, shaking the pan every now and then. Discard any
mussels that have remained shut during cooking.

3 Lift the mussels out of the cooking liquid with a slotted
spoon and divide them between four serving bowls.

4 Strain the cooking liquid into a small pan and add the
tarragon. Boil for a few minutes until reduced a little, check the
seasoning and then pour over the mussels to serve.

Tip... To prepare mussels, scrub off any dirt and remove
any barnacles. Remove the beard, if any, that sticks out
between the shells. Discard any mussels that are already
open or have a cracked shell.

Mediterranean cod bake

Serves 4

289 calories per serving

Takes 15 minutes to prepare,
15 minutes to cook

calorie controlled cooking
  spray

1 yellow pepper, de-seeded
  and sliced

1 green pepper, de-seeded and
  sliced

2 garlic cloves, sliced

400 g can chopped tomatoes

3 heaped tablespoons
  shredded fresh basil

4 x 125 g (4½ oz) skinless cod
  fillets

125 g (4½ oz) mozzarella light,
  torn into pieces

freshly ground black pepper

Serve with 60 g (2 oz) dried tagliatelle per person, cooked according to the packet instructions, as well as some steamed broccoli spears.

1 Preheat the oven to Gas Mark 6/200°C/fan oven 180°C. Lightly spray an ovenproof baking dish with the cooking spray.

2 Heat a non stick frying pan until hot, spray with the cooking spray and cook the peppers and garlic for 4 minutes until browned and starting to soften. Add the tomatoes and basil, season with black pepper and simmer for 3–4 minutes until slightly thickened.

3 Place the cod fillets in the baking dish and pour the sauce over the fish. Scatter the mozzarella over the top and bake for 15 minutes.

Variation... Try other white fish fillets such as hoki or pollock instead of cod – they are often better value than cod and just as tasty.

Crab and coriander linguine

Serves 4

268 calories per serving

Takes 5 minutes to prepare,
  10 minutes to cook

250 g (9 oz) dried linguine

finely grated zest of a lime

juice of 2 limes

**2 x 170 g cans white crab
  meat, drained**

10 cherry tomatoes, halved

**3 tablespoons chopped fresh
  coriander**

**1 red chilli, de-seeded and
  diced**

**salt and freshly ground black
  pepper**

*This is a lovely, fresh tasting pasta dish that would be good
for supper with friends or as a midweek family meal.*

1 Bring a large pan of water to the boil, add the pasta and
cook according to the packet instructions. Drain, reserving
4 tablespoons of the cooking liquid and return both to the pan.

2 Reserving a little coriander and chilli to garnish, add the
remaining ingredients, tossing well to combine. Season and
serve in warm bowls, garnished with the reserved coriander
and chilli.

Variation... This could be made using the same amount of
canned tuna in brine or spring water, drained, instead of
the crab meat.

Mackerel macaroni supper

Serves 4

585 calories per serving

Takes 30 minutes

❄

225 g (8 oz) dried quick cook
macaroni

calorie controlled cooking
spray

225 g (8 oz) courgettes, diced

400 g can chopped tomatoes
with garlic

300 g (10½ oz) peppered
mackerel fillets, skinned and
flaked

4 spring onions, sliced

100 g (3½ oz) half fat mature
Cheddar cheese, grated

*A quick, simple and satisfying supper dish for those days
when you don't have a lot of time to spend in the kitchen.*

1 Bring a large pan of water to the boil, add the pasta and
cook for about 5 minutes until tender. Drain.

2 Meanwhile, heat a large non stick frying pan and spray
with the cooking spray. Add the courgettes to the pan and
cook for 2–3 minutes to soften them.

3 Add the cooked macaroni, tomatoes, mackerel and spring
onions to the pan, stir well and heat through for 5 minutes.

4 Preheat the grill to medium. Spoon the mixture into a
flameproof dish and sprinkle the cheese over the top. Grill for
5 minutes and serve at once.

Tuna with grape salsa

Serves 4
223 calories per serving
Takes 30 minutes

125 ml (4 fl oz) dry white wine
2 teaspoons caster sugar
1 teaspoon Dijon mustard
100 g (3½ oz) white seedless grapes, chopped finely
1 celery stick, diced finely
50 g (1¾ oz) stoned Kalamata olives in brine, drained and chopped finely
1 tablespoon finely chopped fresh parsley
1 tablespoon snipped fresh chives
4 x 125 g (4½ oz) tuna steaks
calorie controlled cooking spray
freshly ground black pepper

This warm salsa is perfect with fresh griddled tuna. Serve with 150 g (5½ oz) cooked polenta per person and steamed mange tout.

1 Put the wine and sugar in a small saucepan and bring to the boil. Simmer for 5 minutes until reduced. Stir in the mustard, grapes, celery, olives, parsley and chives. Season with black pepper and set aside.

2 Meanwhile, heat a griddle pan or non stick frying pan until hot and spray the tuna steaks with the cooking spray. Cook for 6 minutes, turning halfway, until cooked to your liking. Leave to rest for 5 minutes and then serve with the grape salsa.

Spicy cod and sausage kebabs

Serves 4
200 calories per serving
Takes 20 minutes

**200 g (7 oz) skinless cod fillet,
cut into 2.5 cm (1 inch)
cubes**
**450 g (1 lb) low fat pork
sausages, quartered
lengthways**
**2 red peppers, cut into 2.5 cm
(1 inch) squares**

For the sauce
2 tablespoons soy sauce
1 tablespoon clear honey
**1 red chilli, de-seeded
and chopped finely, or
1 teaspoon dried chilli flakes**
1 garlic clove, crushed

*Ideal for the barbecue but also good grilled, these cod
kebabs combine with low fat sausages and red peppers in
a sticky, spicy sauce.*

1 Thread the cod, sausages and red peppers on to eight
skewers, alternating them to look attractive.

2 Mix together the sauce ingredients and place in a shallow
dish long enough to accommodate the skewers. Place
the skewers in the dish and turn until they are completely
covered in the sauce.

3 Preheat the grill or barbecue to high and then lay the
skewers on a piece of foil on the grill pan or put straight on to
the barbecue. Brush with more sauce and grill for 4 minutes.
Turn, brush again and grill for a further 4 minutes until cooked
through.

Tip... If using wooden skewers, soak them in water for
30 minutes beforehand to prevent them from burning.

Cod with orange sauce

Serves 4
190 calories per serving
Takes 30 minutes

**4 x 150 g (5½ oz) skinless cod
fillets**
300 ml (10 fl oz) fish stock
thinly pared zest of an orange
¼ teaspoon turmeric
2 tablespoons light soy sauce
**1 teaspoon chopped fresh
sage or ½ teaspoon dried
sage**
2 tablespoons cornflour
2 tablespoons orange liqueur
225 g (8 oz) fine green beans
freshly ground black pepper

*The orange sauce in this recipe complements the cod
perfectly, as the citrus draws out its flavour.*

1 Place the cod in a large lidded frying pan and pour over the
stock. Add the orange zest and turmeric and bring to the boil.
Reduce the heat, cover and simmer for 10 minutes, until the
fish is cooked through. Remove the fish from the pan and set
aside.

2 Add the soy sauce and sage to the pan and season with
black pepper. Bring to the boil and allow the mixture to bubble
for 2 minutes.

3 Mix the cornflour with the orange liqueur and stir this into
the pan. Cook, stirring, until the sauce thickens. Return the
cod to the pan and heat through for 2 minutes.

4 Meanwhile, bring a pan of water to the boil, add the beans
and cook for 5 minutes. Drain. Serve the fish on a bed of
beans with the sauce spooned over.

Variation... If you prefer not to use liqueur, substitute it with
orange juice.

Cheesy Parmesan prawn bake

Serves 4
278 calories per serving
Takes 20 minutes

225 g (8 oz) dried fusilli
calorie controlled cooking spray
450 g (1 lb) ripe tomatoes, halved
200 g (7 oz) cooked peeled prawns, defrosted if frozen
2 tablespoons capers, chopped roughly
25 g (1 oz) Parmesan cheese, grated finely
salt and freshly ground black pepper
a handful of fresh basil leaves, to garnish

The whole family will love this pasta bake. It really is perfect for a midweek meal.

1 Bring a large pan of water to the boil, add the pasta and cook according to the packet instructions. Drain and keep warm.

2 Meanwhile, heat a large frying pan and spray with the cooking spray. Add the tomatoes and sauté for 3–5 minutes until softened and the juices begin to flow. Preheat the grill to medium.

3 Add the prawns and capers to the tomatoes and heat for 1–2 minutes until hot. Stir into the pasta, mix well and season.

4 Spoon the pasta mixture into a flameproof dish, sprinkle over the Parmesan and grill for 3–5 minutes until bubbling. Serve garnished with the basil leaves.

Almond crusted trout

Serves 4
182 calories per serving
Takes 20 minutes

2 medium slices white or wholemeal bread, torn into small pieces

15 g (½ oz) low fat spread, melted

15 g (½ oz) flaked almonds

4 x 110 g (4 oz) trout fillets

calorie controlled cooking spray

1 red onion, sliced thinly

2 rashers lean back bacon, diced

2 garlic cloves, crushed

1 Savoy cabbage, cored and shredded

salt and freshly ground black pepper

Serve with 100 g (3½ oz) boiled new potatoes per person.

1 Preheat the grill to medium.

2 In a blender or with a hand blender, whizz the bread to crumbs. Mix together with the melted low fat spread and the almonds.

3 Lay out the trout fillets on a grill pan, flesh side up, and season lightly. Press the almond crumb crust on to the trout.

4 Spray a large non stick frying pan or wok with the cooking spray. Stir-fry the onion for 3 minutes over a medium heat to soften. Add the bacon and garlic and cook for 2 minutes until lightly browned. Add the cabbage and 4 tablespoons of water. Stir-fry for 5 minutes until wilted and tender.

5 Meanwhile, grill the trout for 5–6 minutes until it is cooked through and has a crisp golden crust (there is no need to turn over the fish during cooking). Serve the trout with the sautéed cabbage.

Simply vegetarian

Leek and mushroom gratin

Serves 2
100 calories per serving
Takes 10 minutes to prepare,
  15 minutes to cook

calorie controlled cooking
  spray
1 large leek, sliced thinly
125 g (4½ oz) mushrooms,
  sliced thinly
1 large garlic clove, chopped
1 tablespoon light soy sauce
2 tablespoons single cream
1 tablespoon chopped fresh
  parsley
1 tablespoon Parmesan
  cheese, grated
1 tablespoon dried natural
  breadcrumbs
salt and freshly ground black
  pepper

A fantastic light dish that tastes wonderfully indulgent.
Serve with steamed vegetables.

1 Heat a large, lidded, non stick saucepan and spray it with the cooking spray. Add the leek, mushrooms and garlic with 4 tablespoons of water and cook until the mixture sizzles. Cover and cook on a medium heat for 10 minutes, shaking the pan occasionally, until the vegetables have softened.

2 Add the soy sauce and seasoning and then mix in the cream and parsley.

3 Preheat the grill. Divide the leek and mushroom mixture between two flameproof dishes. Mix together the Parmesan cheese and breadcrumbs and then scatter this over the leek and mushrooms.

4 Place the dishes under the preheated grill, until the tops are crisp and golden brown. Cool slightly and serve.

French bread pizza

Serves 4
284 calories per serving
Takes 10 minutes

200 g (7 oz) low fat soft
cheese with garlic and herbs

2 tablespoons reduced fat
pesto

4 x 60 g (2 oz) pieces
French stick, sliced in half
lengthways

150 g (5½ oz) cherry
tomatoes, halved

390 g can artichoke hearts,
drained and quartered

calorie controlled cooking
spray

12 fresh basil leaves, to
garnish

*French bread is an instant base for pizza, so this recipe is
ideal for an easy lunch or light supper.*

1 Preheat the grill to medium. Mix the soft cheese and pesto
together and spread over the bread. Place on the grill pan. Top
with the cherry tomatoes and artichokes and spray with the
cooking spray.

2 Grill for 2–3 minutes until golden and bubbling and serve
garnished with the basil leaves.

Tip... This is a great way to use up day old French bread.

Squash and blue cheese risotto

Serves 2
695 calories per serving
Takes 30 minutes

2 teaspoons olive oil
1 large onion, chopped
2 celery sticks, chopped
450 g (1 lb) winter squash or
    pumpkin, peeled, de-seeded
    and cut into 1 cm (½ inch)
    cubes
200 g (7 oz) dried Italian easy
    cook rice
600 ml (20 fl oz) hot vegetable
    stock
4 sage leaves, torn, or
    ½ teaspoon dried sage
2 tomatoes, de-seeded and
    diced
75 g (2¾ oz) low fat soft
    cheese with garlic and herbs
a handful of chopped fresh
    parsley
salt and freshly ground black
    pepper
50 g (1¾ oz) blue cheese,
    crumbled, to serve

*An interesting array of squashes is available in
supermarkets. This is the ideal recipe for those of you
who have yet to try this interesting vegetable.*

1 Heat the oil in a large, lidded, non stick frying pan and gently
cook the onion and celery until softened. Add the squash or
pumpkin and cook for a further 2 minutes.

2 Stir in the rice and add the hot stock. Cover and simmer for
10–15 minutes, until the stock is nearly absorbed.

3 Stir in the sage, tomatoes, soft cheese and parsley. Season
to taste. Divide between individual bowls and crumble over the
blue cheese.

Tip... Arborio is the classic short stubby grain used to give
risotto its creamy consistency. It does, however, require
more cooking than Italian easy cook rice. This is an
acceptable cheat's version.

Beanie burgers with salsa

Serves 2
137 calories per serving
Takes 20 minutes

❄ (burgers only)

410 g can flageolet or haricot beans, drained and rinsed

1 egg white

½ tablespoon medium curry powder

4 spring onions, chopped

75 g (2¾ oz) carrot, peeled and grated coarsely

calorie controlled cooking spray

2 tomatoes, diced

salt and freshly ground black pepper

These curried bean and vegetable burgers are so easy to make and much tastier than ready-made versions.

1 Tip the beans into a food processor, adding the egg white, curry powder and seasoning. Pulse until mixed, but without processing to a smooth paste.

2 Stir in half the spring onions and all of the grated carrot and mix briefly. Using wet hands, shape the sticky mixture into four burgers.

3 Lightly spray a non stick frying pan with the cooking spray and fry the burgers for 5 minutes on each side over a medium heat.

4 Meanwhile, mix the diced tomatoes with the rest of the spring onions and seasoning. Serve the salsa spooned over the hot burgers.

Breaded garlic mushrooms

Serves 4

170 calories per serving

Takes 10 minutes to prepare,
  20 minutes to cook

15 g (½ oz) plain white flour

**150 g (5½ oz) small chestnut
mushrooms**

**150 g (5½ oz) baby portabello
mushrooms**

2 teaspoons garlic purée

2 eggs, beaten

**100 g (3½ oz) fresh white
breadcrumbs**

**calorie controlled cooking
spray**

1 teaspoon paprika

*Spoil the whole family with this great classic. The
mushrooms can be prepared up to the end of step 3 and
then chilled in the fridge for up to 1 day.*

1 Preheat the oven to Gas Mark 6/200°C/fan oven 180°C.
Put the flour into a large bowl, add all the mushrooms and
toss until coated. It is best to use your hands.

2 Mix together the garlic purée and eggs and put into another
large bowl. Empty the floured mushrooms into the garlic and
egg mixture and toss until coated. Again, it is best to use your
hands.

3 Put the breadcrumbs into the empty flour bowl and drain
away any egg from the mushrooms. Empty the mushrooms into
the breadcrumbs and gently toss until coated.

4 Transfer to a non stick baking tray. Spray with the cooking
spray and bake in the oven for 20 minutes, turning halfway
through until golden and crispy. Sprinkle with the paprika and
serve immediately.

Pea and sweet potato curry

Serves 4
287 calories per serving
Takes 30 minutes

❄ (for up to 1 month)

3 teaspoons cumin seeds
2 teaspoons coriander seeds
2 garlic cloves, chopped
calorie controlled cooking spray
1 large onion, diced
700 g (1 lb 9 oz) sweet potatoes, peeled and chopped
500 ml (18 fl oz) vegetable stock
400 g (14 oz) frozen peas
200 g (7 oz) cottage cheese

A colourful, sweet tasting curry that is also very filling.

1 In a small frying pan, dry fry the cumin and coriander seeds to bring out their flavour. Grind to a paste in a pestle and mortar with the chopped garlic.

2 Heat a large non stick pan, spray with the cooking spray and fry the onion for 4–5 minutes until starting to soften.

3 Add the sweet potatoes and spice paste. Stir well to coat the potatoes with the spicy mixture.

4 Pour in the stock and simmer for 8–10 minutes until the sweet potatoes are nearly cooked.

5 Stir in the peas and cottage cheese and heat through for 1–2 minutes.

Lentil and chick pea casserole

Serves 4
160 calories per serving
Takes 30 minutes

❄

This is a hearty casserole, cooked on top of the stove, containing lentils and spinach. Serve with 1 tablespoon 0% fat Greek yogurt per serving.

calorie controlled cooking spray
1 red onion, sliced thinly
2 garlic cloves, crushed
2 celery sticks, chopped
1 teaspoon cumin seeds
400 g can cherry tomatoes
410 g can green lentils, drained and rinsed
410 g can chick peas, drained and rinsed
1 vegetable stock cube, crumbled
150 g (5½ oz) baby spinach, washed
1 tablespoon chopped fresh parsley, to garnish

1 Lightly spray a large, lidded, non stick saucepan with the cooking spray. Heat until hot and then add the onion and fry for 3 minutes. Add the garlic, celery and cumin and continue cooking in the onion juices for 3 minutes to soften the vegetables.

2 Add the tomatoes, lentils and chick peas with the stock cube and 150 ml (5 fl oz) of water. Bring to the boil, cover and simmer for 10 minutes.

3 Stir in the spinach and cook for a further 2–3 minutes until the spinach has wilted. Serve hot with a sprinkle of parsley on top.

Tip... If you like curry flavours, add 1 tablespoon mild curry powder with the cumin seeds.

Summer vegetable fusilli

Serves 4
335 calories per serving
Takes 20 minutes

This vibrant pasta dish has a wonderfully fresh flavour, with a touch of creamy richness from the half fat crème fraîche. Serve with a large mixed salad.

300 g (10½ oz) dried fusilli
150 g (5½ oz) green beans, halved
150 g (5½ oz) mange tout
calorie controlled cooking spray
2 courgettes, diced
2 garlic cloves, crushed
grated zest of a lemon, plus 1 tablespoon lemon juice
4 tablespoons half fat crème fraîche
4 heaped tablespoons chopped fresh basil
salt and freshly ground black pepper

1 Bring a pan of water to the boil, add the pasta and cook for 7 minutes.

2 Add the green beans and cook for a further 3 minutes, then add the mange tout and cook for 2 minutes more, or until the fusilli is tender.

3 Meanwhile, heat a lidded non stick saucepan, spray with the cooking spray and fry the courgettes for 3–4 minutes until lightly browned. Stir in the garlic and 2 tablespoons of water, season, reduce the heat, cover and cook for 3 minutes or until tender.

4 Drain the pasta and vegetables, reserving 4 tablespoons of the cooking water. Return to the pan and stir in the courgettes, lemon zest and juice, crème fraîche and basil, plus the reserved cooking water. Season well and serve in warmed bowls.

Vegetable pad Thai

Serves 2
431 calories per serving
Takes 25 minutes

125 g (4½ oz) dried rice
   noodles
a kettleful of boiling water
calorie controlled cooking
   spray
1 red onion, sliced thinly
75 g (2¾ oz) mange tout,
   sliced thinly diagonally
75 g (2¾ oz) baby corn, sliced
   thinly diagonally
2 garlic cloves, crushed
1 teaspoon grated fresh root
   ginger
1 red chilli, de-seeded and
   sliced
125 g (4½ oz) beansprouts
1 carrot, peeled and grated
   coarsely
juice of a lime
1 teaspoon light brown soft
   sugar
2 tablespoons soy sauce
1 egg, beaten
3 heaped tablespoons
   chopped fresh coriander
15 g (½ oz) salted peanuts,
   chopped finely, to garnish

It's the combination of salty, sour and sweet ingredients that gives pad Thai its distinctive flavour.

1 Place the noodles in a bowl, cover with boiling water and soak for 4 minutes or according to the packet instructions. Drain and rinse in cold water.

2 Heat a wok or large non stick frying pan until hot and spray with the cooking spray. Add the onion, mange tout, baby corn and 1 tablespoon of water. Stir-fry for 1 minute. Mix in the garlic, ginger and chilli and cook for 1 minute more.

3 Next add the beansprouts, carrot and drained noodles, plus the lime juice, sugar and soy sauce. Toss together for 2 minutes.

4 Drizzle the egg all over the noodle mixture and leave to set for 1 minute before mixing in, adding the coriander. Serve scattered with the peanuts.

Beetroot and caramelised onion tarte tatin

Serves 4
230 calories per serving
Takes 30 minutes

calorie controlled cooking spray
1 onion, sliced very finely
2 tablespoons maple syrup
1 tablespoon balsamic vinegar
200 g (7 oz) cooked beetroot in natural juice, drained and sliced
150 g (5½ oz) ready-to-roll puff pastry
40 g (1½ oz) French medium fat soft goat's cheese
a small handful of wild rocket
salt and freshly ground black pepper

Serve with 100 g (3½ oz) sliced and cooked new potatoes per person, along with a tomato salad.

1 Preheat the oven to Gas Mark 7/220°C/fan oven 200°C. Heat a non stick frying pan and spray with the cooking spray. Add the onions and maple syrup and cook gently for 3 minutes until softened and starting to caramelise. Add the vinegar and cook for 2 minutes longer. Season.

2 Spread one third of the onions in the base of an 18 cm (7 inch) shallow loose-bottomed cake tin. Arrange the beetroot slices in a layer on top. Top with the remaining onions.

3 Roll out the pastry on a piece of non stick baking parchment until just bigger than the cake tin. Put the pastry on top of the onions, tucking in the sides. Bake in the oven for 15 minutes until golden and risen.

4 Upturn on to a plate, dot over the goat's cheese and top with the rocket. Serve immediately.

Spinach and cheese rolls

Serves 4

135 calories per serving

Takes 10 minutes to prepare,
15 minutes to cook

250 g (9 oz) baby spinach,
washed

200 g (7 oz) cottage cheese
with chives

1 tablespoon chopped fresh
dill or 1 teaspoon dried dill

4 x 15 g (½ oz) sheets filo
pastry, measuring
30 x 40 cm (12 x 16 inches)

1 tablespoon low fat spread,
melted

salt and freshly ground black
pepper

*Creamy spinach rolled into light and crispy filo pastry
makes a tasty and attractive meal. Serve these rolls warm
with a green salad and sliced tomatoes.*

1 Bring a pan of water to the boil, add the spinach and cook
for 2–3 minutes. Drain it well, pressing out as much water as
possible.

2 Chop the spinach finely, and then mix it with the cottage
cheese, dill and seasoning.

3 Preheat the oven to Gas Mark 6/200°C/fan oven 180°C.
Using a pastry brush, dab the filo sheets with the melted low
fat spread. Divide the spinach filling into four and place along
the bottom of each sheet, spreading it out to flatten it slightly.
Roll each sheet up firmly, but not too tightly.

4 Place the rolls on a non stick baking tray and bake them for
15 minutes until they are crisp and golden. Slice them in half
and serve them warm.

Variation... This spinach and cottage cheese filling works
brilliantly in jacket potatoes too.

Roasted vegetables with pasta

Serves 4

345 calories per serving

Takes 10 minutes to prepare,
15 minutes to cook

1 large courgette, sliced

1 red onion, sliced

1 red pepper, de-seeded and chopped

100 g (3½ oz) baby corn, halved

100 g (3½ oz) button mushrooms

2 tablespoons olive oil

a few fresh rosemary and thyme sprigs

225 g (8 oz) dried pasta shapes

150 g (5½ oz) virtually fat free plain fromage frais

2 tablespoons finely grated Parmesan cheese

salt and freshly ground black pepper

Roasted vegetables taste delicious stirred through hot pasta.

1 Preheat the oven to Gas Mark 6/200°C/fan oven 180°C.

2 Put all the vegetables into a roasting tin and drizzle with the olive oil. Add the herb sprigs and season. Stir well and roast for about 15 minutes, until just beginning to brown.

3 Meanwhile, bring a pan of water to the boil, add the pasta and cook for about 8–10 minutes until just tender. Drain well, return to the saucepan and add the fromage frais and Parmesan. Heat gently for 2–3 minutes.

4 Fold the hot vegetables through the pasta. Check the seasoning, adding a little more, if needed. Pile on to warmed plates and serve at once.

Vegetable biryani

Serves 4
337 calories per serving
Takes 30 minutes

❄

240 g (8½ oz) dried brown basmati rice
275 g (9½ oz) cauliflower florets
2 carrots, peeled and cut into bite size pieces
175 g (6 oz) frozen petit pois
calorie controlled cooking spray
2 onions, sliced thinly
2 large garlic cloves, chopped
2.5 cm (1 inch) fresh root ginger, grated
1 teaspoon tomato purée
3 tablespoons curry paste
salt and freshly ground black pepper
a handful of chopped fresh coriander, to garnish

This simplified version of a classic Indian dish is lightly spiced and delicious topped with a hard boiled egg per person.

1 Bring a pan of water to the boil, add the rice and cook according to the packet instructions. Drain well.

2 Meanwhile, bring another pan of water to the boil, add the cauliflower and carrots and cook for 3–4 minutes, adding the petit pois for the last minute of cooking time. Drain.

3 Heat a wok or large non stick frying pan and spray with the cooking spray. Add the onions and fry for 6 minutes, stirring frequently. Add the garlic and ginger and cook for another minute. Add the cooked rice and heat through, stirring for 1 minute, and then add the cooked vegetables, tomato purée, curry paste and 5 tablespoons of water.

4 Heat thoroughly, stirring continuously, season well and serve sprinkled with the coriander.

Hallowe'en pumpkin and cashew nut stir-fry

Serves 4
220 calories per serving
Takes 25 minutes

calorie controlled cooking spray

a bunch of spring onions, sliced finely

4 garlic cloves, sliced finely

2 teaspoons coriander seeds, crushed

2 teaspoons mustard seeds

1 kg (2 lb 4 oz) pumpkin, peeled, de-seeded and cut into small chunks

4 tablespoons soy sauce

150 ml (5 fl oz) orange juice

To serve

100 g (3½ oz) unsalted cashew nuts, toasted and chopped

a small bunch of fresh coriander, mint or parsley, chopped

Pumpkin is cheap and plentiful in the autumn, and this recipe really brings out its sweet, satisfying flavour.

1 Heat a lidded wok or large, lidded, non stick pan and spray with the cooking spray. Stir-fry the spring onions, garlic, coriander seeds and mustard seeds for a few minutes, until golden and the mustard seeds begin to pop.

2 Add the pumpkin and soy sauce and stir-fry for 5 minutes more, until the pumpkin is brown on the edges. Add the orange juice, bring to the boil, cover and simmer for 8–10 minutes, until the pumpkin is tender.

3 Scatter with the cashew nuts and fresh herbs to serve.

Margherita pizza

Serves 4

305 calories per serving

Takes 35 minutes to prepare
+ 35 minutes rising,
10–15 minutes to cook

8 tablespoons passata or
   tomato pasta sauce

115 g (4 oz) mozzarella light,
   sliced thinly

2 garlic cloves, chopped finely

a pinch of dried oregano

a handful of fresh basil leaves

1 tablespoon extra virgin
   olive oil

salt and freshly ground black
   pepper

For the pizza dough

7 g sachet dried yeast

a pinch of sugar

350 g (12 oz) strong plain
   white bread flour, plus extra
   for dusting

2 teaspoons olive oil

½ teaspoon salt

*This recipe uses home-made pizza dough, but you could
make this in under 20 minutes with a ready-made 30 cm
(12 inch) pizza base.*

1 Mix the yeast with the sugar and 150 ml (5 fl oz) of warm
water and leave for 10 minutes until frothy. Sift the flour into
a large bowl and make a well in the centre. Pour in the yeast
mixture, oil and salt. Mix together with a palette knife first and
then use your hands until the dough comes together.

2 Tip out on to a floured surface and knead vigorously for
10 minutes. Place in a clean oiled bowl, cover with a damp
tea towel or piece of cling film and leave to rise in a warm
place for 30 minutes until doubled in size.

3 Preheat the oven to Gas Mark 9/240°C/fan oven 220°C.
Punch the dough and push it down and then leave it to rise
again for 5 minutes.

4 Roll out the dough, or stretch it with your fingers, to a 30 cm
(12 inch) circle. Place on a large floured baking tray. For mini
pizzas, divide into four and stretch each to a circle measuring
10 cm (4 inches).

5 Spread the dough with the passata or tomato sauce,
avoiding the edges. Scatter over the cheese, garlic and
herbs and season. Drizzle with the olive oil and bake for
10–15 minutes or until the edges are crisp and golden.

Tip... When kneading the dough it should change in texture
from loose and floury to smooth, soft and elastic. If it
doesn't, then you haven't kneaded long enough or hard
enough.

Stuffed mushrooms

Serves 2
307 calories per serving
Takes 15 minutes to prepare,
10 minutes to cook

4 large flat mushrooms, stalks removed
calorie controlled cooking spray
125 ml (4 fl oz) hot vegetable stock
75 g (2¾ oz) dried couscous
75 g (2¾ oz) frozen sweetcorn or canned sweetcorn, drained
12 cherry tomatoes, halved
15 g (½ oz) sunflower seeds
40 g (1½ oz) half fat mature Cheddar cheese, grated finely
freshly ground black pepper

The sunflower seeds in this colourful dish add a pleasant crunch, which makes a nice contrast to the tender juiciness of the mushrooms.

1 Preheat the oven to Gas Mark 6/200°C/fan oven 180°C.

2 Spray the mushrooms with the cooking spray and season with black pepper. Place on a baking tray, open cup side down, and cook in the oven for 8 minutes.

3 Meanwhile, pour the hot stock over the couscous in a bowl. Cover with a plate and leave to stand for 6–7 minutes to soften. If using frozen sweetcorn, bring a small saucepan of water to the boil and cook the sweetcorn for 2–3 minutes before draining.

4 Add the sweetcorn, tomatoes and half of the sunflower seeds to the couscous and mix together. Remove the mushrooms from the oven and flip them over. Pile the couscous on to the mushrooms and top with the cheese and the rest of the sunflower seeds.

5 Return to the oven for 10 minutes until the cheese is melted and golden.

Tip... Grate hard cheeses such as half fat Cheddar cheese or Parmesan cheese and store them in a food bag in the freezer, ready to use from frozen. You can then easily measure out just what you need.

Quorn and mushroom ragu

Serves 4
342 calories per serving
Takes 30 minutes

❄ (sauce only)

½ x 15 g packet dried porcini
  mushrooms
200 ml (7 fl oz) boiling water
calorie controlled cooking
  spray
1 onion, chopped
2 garlic cloves, crushed
150 g (5½ oz) closed cup
  mushrooms, quartered
400 g can chopped tomatoes
1 teaspoon dried mixed herbs
350 g (12 oz) Quorn mince
250 g (9 oz) dried tagliatelle
freshly ground black pepper

Quorn makes a delicious vegetarian alternative to mince in this tasty ragu.

1 In a small bowl, soak the porcini mushrooms in the boiling water according to the packet instructions.

2 Spray a large, lidded, non stick saucepan with the cooking spray. Add the onion, cover and cook for 4 minutes, adding a splash of water if necessary to prevent it from sticking. Stir in the garlic and mushrooms, cover the pan again and cook for 2–3 minutes more.

3 Add the tomatoes, herbs and black pepper to taste. Tip in the porcini mushrooms and their soaking liquid, except for the very last bit, which may be rather sandy. Stir the Quorn mince into the sauce, cover and simmer for 12 minutes.

4 Meanwhile, bring a pan of water to the boil, add the pasta and cook for 8–10 minutes or according to the packet instructions. Drain and serve topped with the Quorn and mushroom ragu.

Delicious desserts

Chocolate roulade

Serves 6
220 calories per serving
Takes 30 minutes + cooling

✳

calorie controlled cooking
  spray
75 g (2¾ oz) plain white flour
**2 tablespoons unsweetened
  cocoa powder**
3 large eggs
75 g (2¾ oz) caster sugar
**200 g (7 oz) low fat soft
  cheese**
**100 g (3½ oz) virtually fat free
  raspberry fromage frais**
**100 g (3½ oz) raspberries,
  defrosted if frozen**
**2 teaspoons icing sugar, for
  dusting**
**mint leaves, to decorate
  (optional)**

*Roulade is a wonderful dessert that looks and tastes
indulgent but is actually simple to make.*

1 Preheat the oven to Gas Mark 7/220°C/fan oven 200°C.
Spray a 18 x 28 cm (7 x 11 inch) Swiss roll tin with the cooking
spray and line it with greaseproof paper. Spray the paper with
the cooking spray.

2 Sift the flour and cocoa powder into a bowl. Set aside.

3 Break the eggs into a large mixing bowl and add the caster
sugar. Using a hand held electric whisk, whisk them together
until very light and pale in colour. This will take about
5 minutes.

4 Sift the flour and cocoa mixture again, this time into the
whisked mixture. Fold it in gently using a large metal spoon,
not a wooden one. Pour the mixture into the prepared tin and
spread it out to the corners.

5 Bake in the oven for 7–9 minutes, until firm yet springy. Turn
out on to a large sheet of greaseproof paper and then carefully
peel away the lining paper. Cover with a clean, damp tea towel
and leave the sponge until cold.

6 Mix together the soft cheese and fromage frais. Reserve
a few raspberries for decoration and then lightly mash the
remainder with a fork. Stir these into the soft cheese mixture.

7 Trim the edges of the chocolate sponge, fill with the
raspberry mixture and roll it up. Sprinkle with icing sugar and
serve, decorated with mint leaves, if using, and the reserved
raspberries.

Sweet polenta wedges with warm berries

Serves 4

118 calories per serving

Takes 10 minutes +
  15–20 minutes cooling

75 g (2¾ oz) dried polenta

3 tablespoons artificial sweetener

calorie controlled cooking spray

125 g (4½ oz) frozen raspberries

125 g (4½ oz) frozen blueberries

½ teaspoon ground cinnamon, plus extra for dusting

150 g (5½ oz) 0% fat Greek yogurt, to serve

Polenta is usually served as a savoury dish, but it works just as well in this unusual dessert.

1 In a non stick saucepan, bring 300 ml (10 fl oz) of water to the boil. Tip in the polenta and quickly stir until smooth. Cook gently for 2 minutes, stirring occasionally until thickened and similar in consistency to porridge. Stir in 1½ tablespoons of sweetener and then turn the polenta out on to a side plate that has been lightly sprayed with the cooking spray. Smooth the top with the back of a spoon. Leave to cool and set for 15–20 minutes.

2 When cool, cut the polenta into eight wedges, as if a cake. Spray a non stick frying pan with the cooking spray and then fry for 2½ minutes on each side over a high heat, until crisp and golden.

3 Meanwhile, in a lidded saucepan, cook the frozen berries with the cinnamon and remaining sweetener for 5 minutes until juicy and hot.

4 Spoon the warm berries over the crisp polenta wedges and serve topped with the yogurt, sprinkled with a dusting of cinnamon.

Cherry trifles

Serves 4
295 calories per serving
Takes 15 minutes + cooling

450 g (1 lb) fresh cherries
2 tablespoons caster sugar
4 tablespoons cherry brandy
   or sherry
4 trifle sponges
150 ml (5 fl oz) low fat custard
4 tablespoons whipping cream
2 amaretti biscuits, crushed,
   to serve

Make the most of fresh cherries while in season with this easy recipe.

1 Reserve four cherries with stalks. Halve and stone the remaining cherries and put them in a saucepan with the sugar and cherry brandy or sherry. Heat and simmer gently for about 2 minutes, until syrupy. Allow to cool.

2 Place the trifle sponges on four serving plates. Spoon the cooled cherries, with their syrup, over the top. Spoon over an equal amount of custard.

3 Whip the cream in a chilled bowl until it holds its shape and then spoon a little on top of each dessert. Decorate each one with a reserved cherry and sprinkle with crushed amaretti biscuits.

Variations... Try making this dessert with fresh strawberries instead.

You could use low fat aerosol cream instead of fresh whipping cream.

Autumn fruit compôte

Serves 4

80 calories per serving

Takes 20 minutes

2 dessert apples, cored and
  cut into wedges

2 pears, cored and cut into
  wedges

2 plums, stoned and sliced
  into wedges

2 apricots, stoned and sliced
  into wedges

1 cinnamon stick

1 star anise

2 cloves

2 teaspoons artificial
  sweetener

A full flavoured, warming pudding.

1 Place all the ingredients in a saucepan with enough water
to cover.

2 Bring to the boil and then simmer for 10–15 minutes or
until the fruit is soft. Leave to cool or serve warm.

Lemon meringue pots

Serves 4
166 calories per serving
Takes 30 minutes

4 eggs, separated
300 ml (10 fl oz) skimmed milk
finely grated zest of 2 lemons
juice of a lemon
25 g (1 oz) low fat spread
6 teaspoons artificial
  sweetener

These are a quick and easy alternative to a lemon meringue pie.

1 Preheat the oven to Gas Mark 4/180°C/fan oven 160°C.

2 Beat the egg yolks. Bring the milk to the boil in a small saucepan, remove from the heat and add the egg yolks. Return to the heat and cook, stirring continuously until thickened.

3 Stir in the lemon zest, lemon juice and low fat spread. Add 1 teaspoon of artificial sweetener. Spoon the lemon custard into 4 x 150 ml (5 fl oz) ovenproof ramekins and set aside.

4 In a clean, grease-free bowl, whisk the egg whites until stiff peaks form. Sprinkle over the remaining artificial sweetener and whisk to combine. Spoon on top of the lemon custard, spreading it to the edges to seal. Bake for 12–15 minutes until golden and serve immediately.

French apple tarts

Serves 6
160 calories per serving
Takes 15 minutes to prepare,
15 minutes to cook

calorie controlled cooking spray
200 g (7 oz) ready-to-roll puff pastry
1 teaspoon icing sugar
½ teaspoon ground cinnamon
½ teaspoon ground cloves
2 dessert apples e.g. Pink Lady, Fuji or Braeburn
juice of ½ a lemon

Delicious individual little tarts that can be served hot or cold. Great for a dinner party.

1 Preheat the oven to Gas Mark 6/200°C/fan oven 180°C and spray a non stick baking tray with the cooking spray.

2 Roll the pastry out further until it is about 5 mm (¼ inch) thick. Cut into six squares and lay them on the prepared baking tray. Using a sharp knife, score a 2 cm (¾ inch) wide border around each square.

3 Mix the icing sugar, cinnamon and cloves together in a small bowl and place in a small sieve such as a tea strainer.

4 Core the apples and slice thinly, tossing the slices with the lemon juice in a bowl to prevent them from browning. Arrange the apple slices so that they overlap and cover the pastry squares, leaving the border of pastry around each one.

5 Dust each tart with the spiced sugar and bake for 10–15 minutes, or until the pastry is golden brown and risen.

Pear and ginger strudels

Serves 2

228 calories per serving

Takes 10 minutes to prepare,
15 minutes to cook

**411 g can pear halves in
natural juice, drained**

**2 pieces stem ginger in syrup,
diced, plus 2 teaspoons
syrup from the jar**

**2 x 45 g (1½ oz) sheets filo
pastry, measuring
50 x 24 cm (20 x 9½ inches)**

**2 teaspoons low fat spread,
melted**

**calorie controlled cooking
spray**

**½ teaspoon icing sugar, for
dusting**

Serve with 150 g (5 oz) low fat custard per person.

1 Preheat the oven to Gas Mark 6/200°C/fan oven 180°C.
Roughly chop the pears and then pat dry on kitchen towel. Mix
with the diced ginger and ginger syrup.

2 Brush both sheets of filo pastry lightly with the melted low
fat spread and then fold each one in half to make a square.
Spoon half of the pear mixture along the top edge of each filo
square, leaving 5 cm (2 inches) of pastry free at either end.
Fold in the sides of the strudel and roll up, enclosing the filling.

3 Place the strudels on a non stick baking tray sprayed with
the cooking spray and bake for 15 minutes until crisp and
golden. Dust with the icing sugar just before serving.

Banana and peach crumble

Serves 2

314 calories per serving

Takes 10 minutes to prepare,
15 minutes to bake

2 peaches, halved, stoned and
sliced into wedges

1 banana, sliced

50 g (1¾ oz) plain wholemeal
flour

25 g (1 oz) low fat spread

25 g (1 oz) light brown soft
sugar

*Banana and peaches are a wonderful combination,
especially when topped with this simple crumble.*

1 Preheat the oven to Gas Mark 5/190°C/fan oven 170°C.
Place the peach wedges and banana slices in the bottom of a
600 ml (20 fl oz) ovenproof dish. Add 3 tablespoons of water.

2 Place the flour in a bowl and rub in the low fat spread until it
resembles breadcrumbs. Stir in the sugar.

3 Spoon the crumble mixture over the fruit and bake for
15 minutes until golden.

Mango and passion fruit mousses

Serves 8
116 calories per serving
Takes 15 minutes

3 large ripe mangos
300 g (10½ oz) low fat soft cheese
3–4 teaspoons artificial sweetener
3 egg whites
6 passion fruits, halved

A light and tangy mousse with the added crunch of passion fruit seeds.

1 Cut down the sides of the stone of the mangos and then cut off the skin. Remove any more flesh that you can from the stones before discarding them. Roughly chop the flesh and place in a food processor or use a hand blender. Blend to a purée. Add the soft cheese and sweetener to taste and blend again.

2 In a clean, grease-free bowl, whisk the egg whites until they form stiff peaks. Place the mango mixture in a bowl and carefully fold in the egg whites.

3 Scoop the flesh and seeds from the passion fruits. Using eight serving glasses, layer the mango mix with a spoonful of passion fruit. Repeat, ending with the passion fruit. Serve immediately.

Tip... Try to buy ripe mangos – not too firm but with a bit of give to the flesh, as they have a better flavour and are naturally sweeter.

Fruity cinnamon rice pudding

Serves 2
254 calories per serving
Takes 20 minutes

75 g (2¾ oz) dried risotto rice
300 ml (10 fl oz) skimmed milk
¾ teaspoon ground cinnamon
60 g (2 oz) dried apricots, diced
1 tablespoon caster sugar

A quick hob-cooked version of rice pudding, flavoured with sweet cinnamon.

1 Place the rice in a non stick saucepan with the milk, cinnamon and 100 ml (3½ fl oz) of water. Bring to the boil, stirring occasionally so that the rice doesn't stick to the base of the pan, especially towards the end of the cooking time.

2 Simmer for about 18 minutes until most of the liquid has been absorbed and the rice is tender. It should have a soft, slightly soupy consistency when ready.

3 Just before serving, stir in the apricots and sugar.

Raspberry and melon crush

Serves 4
55 calories per serving
Takes 20 minutes

250 g (9 oz) frozen raspberries
½ ripe honeydew melon

This luscious dessert is so easy to prepare and refreshing.
Wonderful on a summer's evening.

1 Tip the raspberries into a food processor and leave them for about 15 minutes, until they start to thaw but remain half frozen.

2 Meanwhile, scoop out the seeds from the melon. Peel it and cut it into chunks. Add the melon to the food processor and blend with the raspberries until the fruit becomes slushy.

3 Spoon the crush into glasses or individual bowls and serve immediately.

Baked strawberry Alaskas

Serves 4
194 calories per serving
Takes 20 minutes

4 x 25 g (1 oz) slices jam
Swiss Roll

1 ripe peach or nectarine,
skinned and stoned

2 tablespoons sherry

250 g (9 oz) strawberries,
sliced thinly, reserving
4 whole strawberries to
garnish

1 egg white

50 g (1¾ oz) caster sugar

4 x 60 g (2 oz) scoops low fat
vanilla ice cream

Soft chewy meringue hides an ice cream and fruit centre on a jam and sponge base.

1 Preheat the grill to high. Place the Swiss Roll slices in the bottom of four small ramekin dishes.

2 Mash or liquidise the peach or nectarine with the sherry. Spoon the purée over the sponge bases and top with the sliced strawberries.

3 In a clean, grease-free bowl, whisk the egg white until it forms stiff peaks. Whisk in the sugar, a little at a time, until the meringue becomes glossy.

4 Spoon a scoop of ice cream on top of the sliced strawberries and then swirl the meringue on top. Make sure that the meringue forms a seal, without gaps, around the edge of each ramekin dish to insulate the ice cream from the heat.

5 Quickly heat under the grill until the meringue is tinged golden brown. Top each with a whole strawberry and serve immediately.

Roasted stuffed peaches

Serves 4

97 calories per serving

Takes 10 minutes to prepare, 20 minutes to cook

2 peaches

150 ml (5 fl oz) orange juice

60 g (2 oz) ricotta cheese

1 tablespoon icing sugar, sifted

½ teaspoon vanilla extract

25 g (1 oz) amaretti biscuits, crushed roughly

Ensure the fruit is ripe so that the roasted peaches will be sweet and juicy.

1 Preheat the oven to Gas Mark 5/190°C/fan oven 170°C. Halve and stone the peaches and place cut side up in a snug fitting ovenproof dish. Pour the orange juice into the dish so that the peaches sit in the juice.

2 Beat together the ricotta cheese, icing sugar and vanilla extract. Divide the mixture between the holes in the peaches. Scatter over the amaretti biscuits and bake for 20 minutes until softened. Serve one peach half each with some of the juice from the dish.

Variations... If you are not keen on amaretti biscuits, use 40 g (1½ oz) reduced fat crushed digestive biscuits instead.

You can use ripe nectarines or plums instead of the peaches.

Zabaglione with raspberries

Serves 4
220 calories per serving
Takes 15 minutes

4 egg yolks
75 g (2¾ oz) caster sugar
100 ml (3½ fl oz) Marsala wine or sweet sherry
150 g (5½ oz) raspberries

This warming mousse should be served in small glasses as it is very rich. Serve with two amaretti biscuits each.

1 Place the egg yolks, sugar and Marsala or sherry in a large bowl (the mixture will more than double in volume). Place the bowl over a pan of gently simmering water. Whisk the mixture until it is pale and very thick – it is easiest to do this with an electric whisk. It may take as long as 10 minutes.

2 Pour the warm foam into four small wine or shot glasses.

3 Drop the raspberries into the foam and serve immediately.

Blueberry pies

Serves 4
148 calories per serving
Takes 15 minutes

25 g (1 oz) granulated sugar
450 g bag frozen blueberries
250 ml (9 fl oz) apple juice
2 teaspoons cornflour
4 x 20 g slices Weight
    Watchers White Danish
    sliced bread, crusts removed

Using store cupboard and freezer ingredients, these quick assembly pies are the ideal last minute solution. Serve with 1 tablespoon of light single cream per person.

1 Reserve 2 teaspoons of sugar and put the rest in a saucepan along with the blueberries and apple juice. Heat gently until the sugar has dissolved and the blueberries have just defrosted, about 3 minutes. Using a slotted spoon, remove the blueberries and divide between four 200 ml (7 fl oz) ramekins.

2 In a small bowl, dissolve the cornflour in 1 tablespoon of cold water and then add to the juice in the saucepan. Bring to the boil, stirring, and cook for 1 minute until thickened. Carefully pour equal amounts of the thickened juice mixture over the blueberries in the ramekins.

3 Preheat the grill to medium. Cut each slice of bread into four strips and arrange four strips on top of each ramekin in a lattice pattern. Sprinkle with the reserved sugar and place under the grill for 1–2 minutes until golden. Serve immediately.

Variation... For something different, use other frozen fruit, such as 450 g (1 lb) Black Forest fruits.

Blackberry and apple delight

Serves 2

98 calories per serving

Takes 20 minutes to prepare +
  10 minutes cooling

25 g (1 oz) dried tapioca,
  rinsed

330 ml can diet cream soda

1 ginger herbal tea bag

100 g (3½ oz) blackberries

1 eating apple, cored and
  sliced thinly

2 tablespoons virtually fat free
  plain fromage frais

*Tapioca is a pearl-like grain that can be found near the
pasta and grains in most large supermarkets.*

1 Put the tapioca, cream soda and tea bag into a small pan.
Gently bring to the boil and simmer on a very low heat for
5 minutes. Add the blackberries and simmer for a further
5–10 minutes until cooked. Remove from the heat and leave
to cool for 10 minutes.

2 Discard the tea bag, squeezing out the juices, and serve
the tapioca in bowls, topped with the apple slices and
fromage frais.

Strawberry and hazelnut strata

Serves 4

206 calories per serving

Takes 10 minutes to prepare,
8 minutes to cook

**40 g (1½ oz) fresh white
breadcrumbs**

25 g (1 oz) demerara sugar

15 g (½ oz) chopped hazelnuts

**300 g (10½ oz) strawberries,
sliced**

1 tablespoon icing sugar

**500 g carton low fat custard,
chilled**

*The toasted hazelnut and crumb mixture adds a tasty
crunch factor to this layered dessert.*

1 Preheat the oven to Gas Mark 4/180°C/fan oven 160°C.

2 Mix the breadcrumbs with the sugar and hazelnuts and
spread out on a tray lined with non stick baking parchment.

3 Bake for 8 minutes, stirring halfway through, until the
crumbs are caramelised and crisp. Set aside to cool. Mix the
strawberries with the icing sugar to sweeten.

4 Layer the chilled custard, strawberries and crunchy hazelnut
crumbs into four dessert glasses or bowls. Serve immediately.

Index

Other titles in the Weight Watchers Mini Series

ISBN 978-0-85720-932-0

ISBN 978-0-85720-935-1

ISBN 978-0-85720-934-4

ISBN 978-0-85720-938-2

ISBN 978-0-85720-931-3

ISBN 978-0-85720-937-5

ISBN 978-0-85720-936-8

ISBN 978-0-85720-933-7

ISBN 978-1-47111-084-9

ISBN 978-1-47111-089-4

ISBN 978-1-47111-091-7

ISBN 978-1-47111-087-0

ISBN 978-1-47111-090-0

ISBN 978-1-47111-085-6

ISBN 978-1-47111-088-7

ISBN 978-1-47111-086-3

For more details please visit www.simonandschuster.co.uk